Child of Grace

A Death Row Story

DR. CHRIS BROWN

ISBN 978-1-64416-274-3 (paperback)
ISBN 978-1-64416-275-0 (digital)

Copyright © 2018 by Dr. Chris Brown

All rights reserved. No part of this publication may be reproduced, distributed, or transmitted in any form or by any means, including photocopying, recording, or other electronic or mechanical methods without the prior written permission of the publisher. For permission requests, solicit the publisher via the address below.

Christian Faith Publishing, Inc.
832 Park Avenue
Meadville, PA 16335
www.christianfaithpublishing.com

Holy Bible, New International Version®, NIV® Copyright ©1973, 1978, 1984, 2011 by Biblica, Inc.® Used by permission. All rights reserved worldwide.

Printed in the United States of America

CONTENTS

Acknowledgments 5
Preface..7
Chapter 1: It Had to Start Somewhere...............11
Chapter 2: Crime and Punishment 31
Chapter 3: Hope in the Darkness.......................53
Chapter 4: The Wrong Direction.......................70
Chapter 5: Into the Light...................................90
Chapter 6: Ain't Got Time to Die 110
Chapter 7: Politics Become Personal 128
Chapter 8: A Different Kind of Freedom 147
Chapter 9: My Life After His Death 162
Afterword...177
Notes 181

ACKNOWLEDGMENTS

It would be impossible to acknowledge every person who has been part of my journey, but I must take a moment to mention a few people who have helped tremendously with this project. First and foremost, all thanks and all glory go to my Lord and Savior Jesus Christ, through whom all things are possible. My beautiful wife, Sarah, through her infinite patience with me, also made this possible. My precious children, Emily and Joseph, give me inspiration every day to be the best I can be. Sarah Annerton, prayed, encouraged, reviewed an early draft of the book, and gave of her time and incredible talent to create the artwork for this book. My good friends Andrew Isley and Garrett Smith spent a great deal of time reading and providing feedback to make the writing much better than I am capable of on my own. My editor, Jennifer Kelly, helped put the polish on the final product, just as she did for my dissertation some years ago.

ACKNOWLEDGMENTS

And, finally, my Kairos teammates and my brothers in white are always full of encouragement and affirmation.

PREFACE

"You need to write a book."

I'm sure many would-be authors receive that encouragement. I doubt many of them receive that encouragement in prison. It was my second experience volunteering with Kairos Prison Ministry, and I had just finished giving a twenty-minute talk on "Obstacles to Accepting God's Grace." The main theme of the talk was that no one is beyond the reach of God's grace. It was a theme that was well received inside prison, both among the Kairos team and the men in white, as we call the inmates. A man in white, whose velvet voice left no doubt about his previous occupation in the radio business, was adamant. "You need to write a book. I've never heard a story like that from the child's perspective. You've got to write it." Clearly, he made an impression. I had thought about writing my dad's story, the part of my talk that really captivated this audience, several times over the years. I had never thought about writing this story

PREFACE

from my own perspective. Writing it from my perspective seemed much less daunting. As weeks went by, I simply could not take my mind off it. With time and much prayer, I decided the Holy Spirit was really leading me to write this book. It would be just like my Savior to use a prison inmate as the spark for this endeavor.

My dad's name was Gary Brown. What made his story so captivating for a room full of prison inmates is that he too was a man in white almost the entire time I knew him. It was not his first time in prison, but a judge and a jury sentenced him to Alabama's death row when I was six years old. He was executed when I was a senior in college, age twenty-two. Not long after the crime that landed him on death row, he accepted Jesus as his Lord and Savior. Jesus loves to use the least among us, and my dad became a force for the kingdom of God. He went to his earthly death confident in where he would end up for eternity, and his relentless witness meant many people will join him there.

If you ask me to sum up the entire Bible with one word, that word would be *redemption*. Jesus Christ was the ultimate redeemer, engaged in the ultimate act of redemption to save all God's children. Followers of Jesus are merely children of grace. The simplest definition of grace is the free and unmerited favor of God. In Christ's death on the cross, He showed that His grace and love for us know no limits. Nothing anyone can do is so bad or so extreme that God's grace can't reach and redeem them.

That's what this book is really about. It is partly my story and partly my dad's story, but it is all part of the grand story of God's grace. I hope Jesus, Gary, and my friends in white are all pleased with it.

CHAPTER 1

It Had to Start Somewhere

> For you created my inmost
> being; you knit me together
> in my mother's womb.
> —Psalm 139:13 (NIV)

I wasn't born in jail, but I came pretty close. Dad was in jail in a small city outside of Birmingham, Alabama. Despite being in early labor, my mom was too stubborn to leave him in jail, wanting to bail him out before giving birth. In the afternoon hours of November 11, 1980, a hapless young deputy was on duty at the jail, and he didn't have the authority to release someone on bail. Only the sheriff could do that, and he wouldn't be in for a while. My mom, eighteen years old at the time, escorted there by her dad, Billy, to bail out her twenty-two-year-old husband, wouldn't budge. The deputy pleaded with Billy to talk some sense into her, but Billy just laughed at the thought that she would listen to him or anybody else.

I have to feel a bit sorry for the young deputy; his adherence to the rules nearly led him to be part of delivering a teenage girl's baby. Knowing my mom, delivering the baby would have been easier than arguing with her. Fortunately for everyone involved, the sheriff did show up, and my mom posted bail. The whole crazy family vacated the jail and made it to St. Vincent's Hospital in Birmingham in time for me to have an ordinary hospital birth the following day.

By the time I was old enough to hear that story, nobody remembered exactly what my dad had been arrested for. It would be safe to assume it involved alcohol, drugs, fast cars, or, most likely, all of the above. Getting police attention for some combination of those things was a common occurrence from the time he was old enough to drive until his final arrest. The impending arrival of a child had no deterrent effect on that behavior; in fact, the presence of his only child did not deter any of his actions over the next several years. Before I turned one, my parents had separated, my mom citing the fact that he kept partying just as hard after having a son as the main reason for the split. They would remain friends and were even roommates at one point after they divorced. My mom was also not a model citizen by any measure, and by my third birthday, my paternal grandparents had custody of me.

One of my earliest memories is standing in their living room with my blue suitcase. It is not so much a coherent memory as it is a single image coupled with feelings of fear and confusion. I didn't understand what was happening; I just knew there was a major change in my life. In an almost literal sense, I was rescued by my grandparents, but I would be much older before I truly understood that. They answered God's call to take me in.

Visiting a maximum security prison like Holman Correctional Facility, where Alabama's death row is located, is quite an experience. I grew up visiting this facility, so I never thought much about it. However, when I saw the reaction others had on their first visit, I realized the whole thing could be traumatic. The approach from the highway was through a gate that was always open during visiting hours and then down a half mile of rough road that went past the prison's farm fields. That program was later cancelled, but

IT HAD TO START SOMEWHERE

for many years, I saw the general population inmates working the fields as we drove in to the prison. The parking lot was little more than a patch of gravel at the time my dad got there, with a large tower in the middle with armed guards who controlled access to the front gate. The prison was surrounded by a very tall double-layer fence with several rows of razor wire. The men were able to play basketball and volleyball during their exercise time, and many a ball was lost to the razor wire after an errant shot. When we arrived at the prison, we stood at the gate, waiting for the tower guards to buzz us through. We would enter the first gate, which would have to completely close before they would open the second gate and let us through. For a brief moment, between these gates, we were literally in a cage. Whenever a first-time visitor was with us, I quickly discerned their tension during that brief moment. From there, we walked down a sidewalk along the outside of an administrative building before entering the building that held the visitation yard and some other offices and facilities.

Every visitor signed in at the entrance to the visitation yard. The prison allowed each inmate a short list of eight adults who were approved to visit. Inmates could update the list about every six months, and once or twice a year, they could apply for a "special visit" for someone outside their list, like a distant relative or a friend who wanted to visit. The prison's rules forced Dad into a game to rotate people who wanted to see him on and off the list at the right times. At least one visitor had to be an adult, which, in Alabama, means nineteen years old. I was seventeen when I moved away from home and started college, so that age restriction became a bit awkward. I had a college girlfriend who was a little older than me, and Dad put her on his list for a while so we could visit on our own. Dad had some friends with little or no family who visited them; he put some of our extended family on their lists so everyone could visit. The rules didn't allow mixed visits, but if we happened to all sit close together and intermingle a bit, no one seemed to mind. This scheme was how I got to know some of the other men on death row.

After visitors signed in at the front desk, a corrections officer of the same gender searched us. Each of us would get a thorough pat down, including removing our shoes so our feet could be checked. The pat down was another moment in which the tension was visible on the faces of first-time visitors. The prison allowed us to take in only identification and up to ten dollars in change for the vending machines. I had many a vending machine sandwich during my time visiting there, though I never mastered getting food at the temperature I wanted from those microwaves. For many years, the prison allowed the men to take vending machine items from the yard back to their cells, so there was another game to see how much change the combined visiting group could bring in and how many items we could buy for Dad to take back with that change. The prisoners had a "store" that came around the cell block regularly from which they could buy drinks or snacks, but the vending machines on the visiting yard held more variety. They also had cigarette machines, and although Dad had quit smoking by the time he was there, he always took a couple of packs back to use as currency.

After the check-in and pat down process, a noisy motorized gate would open and allow us into the inner part of the building. The visiting yard itself was enclosed all the way around with narrow ventilation windows that were typically tilted slightly open. The hallways around the visiting yard were often quite noisy, particularly because of clanging gates on either side. The visitation room was a bit below the level of the surrounding hallways; visitors walked down a short ramp and through a glass door to enter. Once, a cart had gotten away from someone and broken the glass door; four corrections officers had to sit there on guard for the whole day. The sergeant who worked that area for the first several years Dad was there was a short blonde woman in her sixties. She didn't look like she could physically stop anyone from doing anything, but she had one of those looks that kept every prisoner in line. No visitor or inmate entered or left the room without her permission.

The visitation room was roughly forty feet by forty feet, filled with single-piece table and chair sets with four uncomfortable seats and brown metal benches with cushions on them around the outside. Near the end of my time visiting there, the benches were made off-limits because someone had been caught trying to sneak drugs in using the cushions. After that, it was uncomfortable wooden seats for everyone. The open arrangement of the room is what allowed us to mix the visitor lists some and still give everyone a chance to see each other. Each corner of the room held an industrial fan, since this space had no air conditioning just like the cell blocks and most of the prison. With the hallway noise, the fans, and a yard full of visitors, visits were a constant cacophony of noise. In the back of the room were steps up to the door where the inmates came through. They had a bathroom back there that they would visit periodically. Each visit had a moment of anticipation as we waited for the back door to open and the men to come through. They would be uncuffed and allowed to enter one at a time. There was always a chance Dad, for some reason, might not be allowed to come. It never happened to us, but a few times, we did see other people wait only to find out their incarcerated family member had been disallowed from visiting for some reason.

That noisy room was where I got to spend all my time with my dad. That was where I got to know him, share my life with him, and learn all about his life.

Dad was born on July 14, 1958, in Birmingham, Alabama. He was the third of four children, with two older sisters, Barbara and Nancy, and a younger brother, Leonard. His parents, who became my adoptive parents, were typical working-class people. My granddad, my dad, and I share the middle name Leon, which is what my granddad went by. My mom hated that name, but when I was born on my granddad's birthday, she felt like she had to give me the same middle name. The elder Leon came from a poor family in rural northeast Alabama and, like almost everyone else of his generation, went off to fight in World War II as soon as he finished high school. He was a real war hero who fought in the Pacific with the Army's famed Americal Division, took part in multiple battles and at least one amphibious landing, was wounded multiple times, and, several decades later, would posthumously receive the Bronze Star Medal. He moved to the city after the war, met my grandmother, Sara, and married her less than six months later. Sara also came from a poor family and grew up on the outskirts of Birmingham. Her name was spelled Sarah on her birth certificate. Nobody remembers when she changed it, but my granddad used to joke that she lost the *h* in the Great Depression because she didn't have anything else to lose. She dropped out of school in ninth grade to help support her family and the war effort by sewing ammunition bags. By the time my dad was born, Leon was well into an almost forty-year career in the coal industry, working in a chemical lab at a plant that made coke, a byproduct of coal. My grandmother kept a home-based daycare and spent a great deal of time volunteering at the Southern Baptist church they would attend for more than half a century. Leon and Sara were characteristic salt-of-the-earth people who did everything they could for their family and showed up at church every time the doors were open. Unlike so many cases, my dad's spiral into darkness did not begin with an abusive family life or a rough upbringing. He was raised in a Christian home; he just turned away from the values with which he was raised.

Dad was a typical child up through junior high school. He made good grades, played baseball and basketball, and didn't get in much trouble. By that time, the Birmingham area had seen the collapse of the steel industry and had become high in poverty and crime; it had become the Southern equivalent of the Midwestern Rust Belt cities. It was easy to find drugs, alcohol, and all kinds of criminal behavior. Around age fourteen, Dad tried a little wine and then smoked marijuana for the first time. Thus began his downward spiral into the lifestyle of an addict. For about a year after he first tried it, he smoked marijuana once or twice a month. Then he had an epiphany: if he started selling it, he could smoke it a lot more often. Of course, his grades suffered as he cared less and less about school. When he was in the tenth grade, his mom found some marijuana in his drawer at home. The same day, he had gotten suspended from school for cutting class. He got home with his pink slip from school only to find Leon home from work early to talk to him about the marijuana. My dad promised them he wouldn't smoke anymore, but he had no intention of keeping that promise. That moment was the first of many warnings and wake-up calls that might have made my dad change his course. The apostle Paul wrote in First Corinthians 10:13 (NIV), "No temptation has overtaken you except what is common to mankind. And God is faithful; he will not let you be tempted beyond what you can bear. But when you are tempted, he will also provide a way out so that you can endure it." God always provides a way out; He provided many ways out over the years that my dad refused to take.

When I was old enough, sitting in that noisy room at Holman, Dad would tell me more about all the events that led him there. That visiting yard was the context and backdrop for everything he told me. The stories of his life after that empty promise to stop smoking marijuana got more and more extreme. He had numerous near-death experiences, but none of them even slowed him down on the highway to destruction. The theme over the next decade of Dad's life was, time after time, God supernaturally saved him and gave him opportunities to turn his life around. Dad had left his old friends and girlfriend behind so he could jump headlong into the lifestyle of sex, drugs, and rock and roll. Not long after his promise

IT HAD TO START SOMEWHERE

to stop smoking marijuana, Dad and some of his new friends found a bottle of Valium that belonged to one of their mothers. He and two friends took the entire bottle of Valium, about twenty pills each. They didn't know much about drugs at that point and had no idea how large a dose that was. His friends quickly passed out, but somehow, Dad maintained consciousness and went looking for more pills. Instead of medication, he found rat poison pills, which he took. After taking twenty Valiums and then an unknown amount of rat poison, he took his friend's car and drove to his girlfriend's house. Dad was so wasted that his girlfriend made him leave before her parents saw him. Miraculously, he made it back to the house next door to where he'd started from without killing himself or anyone else. He didn't remember it, but as he turned right onto the street where he had started this misadventure, he passed out, the steering wheel still turning, and slowly rolled into a tree in the neighboring yard. Two people he knew from school were at that house and came outside to see what had happened. They eventually figured out where Dad had been and went next door to discover the other two passed-out kids, the empty Valium bottle, and the empty rat poison bottle. It didn't take a detective to figure out what had happened. They called for help, and Dad was rushed to the hospital to get his stomach pumped. A couple of days later, he woke up in the hospital with his mom standing over him. Dad could easily have died from this mistake, but in His grace, God saved him.

"Did you even consider quitting drugs after that?"

The answer to my question was no, not really. That binge on Valium and rat poison might have slowed some people down, but not my dad. A few weeks later, he got caught with 60 hits of methamphetamines and 120 barbiturates at school. A sheriff found the drugs under his car. He was sixteen years old at the time. He made a deal to tell them who he had gotten the drugs from in exchange for the charges against him being dropped. Predictably, what he actually gave them was a false name, false description of a man, and a false description of his car. Surprisingly, they believed his story, and the judge dropped the case. He could have easily landed in juvenile detention for the rest of his high school years after being caught with that amount of drugs or being caught in an obvious lie to the sheriff and the judge.

When Dad started high school, the only thing he cared about in school was the band. He loved music and had been the first chair drummer in seventh and eighth grades. By ninth grade, he was in the high school's marching band. He loved playing at the football games and being on the field for the excitement of the game. Football was and still is huge in Alabama; even high school games are major events. Halfway through the tenth grade, with drugs his new passion in life, he stopped caring about anything else, including the marching band and the thrill of the football games. He was in a little rock-and-roll band by then, so he kept playing the drums in that band and gave up the only thing keeping him in school. By the end of his tenth-grade year, he had quit school altogether. He moved in with Nancy, the younger of his sisters, and her husband, James, for a while after he quit school, spending his time selling and smoking marijuana and experimenting with harder drugs. Both of his big sisters did some hard partying in those days, but Nancy and James were both deeply entrenched in that lifestyle. Much later, she would feel tremendous guilt about having enabled my dad's addictions and being a part of his downward spiral. It is unfair, but the family always feels some measure of guilt and wonders what might have been different.

When Dad first turned sixteen and received his temporary driver's license, my granddad had planned to buy him a car. It was a 1968 Mustang 2+2, a hot car then and now. Dad found a way to mess up that deal. He got high and took his mom's car, joyriding with a couple of girls. He was driving fast in an area he didn't know well and came to a T-intersection. He couldn't make the turn, hit the curb, and bent a tie-rod. The car couldn't be driven away at that point. There was no hiding it, so he had to call his dad. When my granddad got there, he tore up Dad's temporary driver's license and threw it away, along with his plans to buy that Mustang. A year later, after my dad had lived with Nancy and James for a little while, Leon enticed him to come back home and go to summer school with the promise of a car. He got a Mercury Montego—not bad, but definitely not as nice as that Mustang. Back at home and back in school, Dad once again had the opportunity to turn his life around before it got any worse. He struggled through the eleventh grade and barely passed. As he started twelfth grade, he was still taking two classes from that prior school year He also continued to drink and do drugs, often skipping class to engage in those activities. The principal caught him cutting class for about the fifth time that year and said Dad would be suspended.

IT HAD TO START SOMEWHERE

Dad's reply was, "No, I won't because I quit." With that pronouncement, he ended his high school education. He did get his GED about a year later under pressure from his mom. He was high when he took the exam and was fortunate he passed it.

"After I dropped out, I really thought I was free," Dad told me. "But it was that fake kind of freedom where you think you can do anything you want, but you're just enslaved to the drugs." Without the burden of school, he went to work at a local car dealership, cleaning and preparing cars for delivery. He got an apartment with a friend and started shooting up heroin for the first time. He was out of the house and out of school and had nothing holding him back from the lifestyle he thought he wanted. "In my drugged-out mind, life was good— working a decent job, using drugs, selling drugs, and having different women over all the time." He talked my granddad into loaning him enough money to buy a motorcycle, and less than a month later, he was in a serious accident that left him with a compound fracture in his leg. This was another one of several near-death experiences he had involving vehicles and drugs. As it turned out, the other party was considered to be at fault, and her insurance paid Dad's salary and bills. "In my twisted mind, I thought this was great—using legal drugs from the doctor and the illegal drugs I was already taking and not having to go to work." Eventually, he recovered and went back to work at the car dealership; this time, as the man in charge of maintenance for the used vehicles. He was selling marijuana to the sales manager and most of the sales staff, so he had free run of the place. One night, he borrowed one of the used cars, as he often did, and drove around with a friend after shooting up liquid barbiturates. He passed out with the car stopped on the road. When he woke up, the car was still in drive, and his foot was on the brake. It was a miracle he hadn't even idled down the road and hit something, but moments after he drove off, he passed out again and went straight off the side of the road at a curve. The car was totaled, but he made up a story about being run off the road and got away with it. He even had a friend who got his rolling papers and syringe out of that car before anybody at the dealership found them. That job finally came to an end when they found a shotgun in the trunk of a used car while showing it to a customer. "They thought I had been out robbing places in the used cars," Dad told me. "The shotgun wasn't mine, and I hadn't robbed anybody, but I couldn't blame them for thinking maybe I had."

IT HAD TO START SOMEWHERE

No job lasts long for a drug addict.

My dad was always the one nominated to drive while drunk or high. "I don't think I was any less messed up than the others, but maybe I was just better at driving wasted or maybe they wanted me to be the one in the most trouble if we got caught." He had talked Leon into cosigning on a car loan for a nice Gran Torino Sport. My granddad had no desire to enable all of Dad's bad behavior. Instead, he was just doing everything he could to try and get Dad to step away from the drugs. As usual, it didn't take my dad long to destroy that car. Like jobs, cars don't last long in the hands of an addict. Dad and three friends were driving around completely wasted; he was doing about ninety miles per hour over a hill when he hit a patch of gravel that had not been there before. The car flew off the road, rolled one complete time in the air, landed on two trees, rolled off the trees, and landed on the car's roof. The three passengers only had scrapes and bruises, but Dad was caught half out of the car with one leg underneath the vehicle. He had broken the same bone, this time on the opposite leg, as he had in his earlier motorcycle crash.

My grandmother saw the vehicle and the scene of the crash, and the first thing she said to him in the hospital was, "Son, the Lord must be saving you for something because you should have been dead." It would not be the last time she said that to him. This was the theme of Dad's life.

Once again, Dad completely ignored the warning sign of this drug-produced near-death experience. "I was like that AC/DC song—'no stop signs, speed limit, nobody's gonna slow me down.'" After that wreck, he tricked the doctor into giving him more pain medication than he really needed; this time, getting his high from legal medication. Dad ended up getting a settlement check from the previous motorcycle crash for five thousand dollars that let him pay back some debts. He paid my granddad back for the times he had been bailed out of jail. At one point, Dad was so brazen and shameless that he had posed as Leonard at the bank, stealing four hundred dollars from his little brother's savings account; he paid back that money with the settlement check as well. He paid off his car note from the Gran Torino, put some money down on a new apartment, and still had enough money left over to buy drugs.

With a new apartment and plenty of money for drugs, Dad and his friends had a big party with methamphetamines and PCP (Phencyclidine). News of a big party gets around fast, and several people from the apartment complex showed up. Dad met a

IT HAD TO START SOMEWHERE

girl who caught his eye, so he asked if she wanted to do some methamphetamines with him. She said yes, but she wanted to shoot up rather than snort. He happily obliged and got her high. It turned out it was the first time she had ever shot up drugs. Dad really liked her even though she was somewhat shy. He was nineteen, and she was only fifteen. That was how he met my mom.

CHAPTER 2

Crime and Punishment

> In him we have redemption through his blood, the forgiveness of sins, in accordance with the riches of God's grace.
> —Ephesians 1:7 (NIV)

Unlike my dad, my mom did not grow up in a good home. Both of her parents were alcoholics, and they divorced when she was young. Mom was the oldest of three girls, though there was only about a year between each of them. After their parents divorced, the youngest sister, Sandra, stayed with their dad for a while and eventually ended up with an aunt. My mom and her middle sister, Mary, stayed with their mom, Jean, who was quite the partier in her own right and did little to care for them. My mom is severely dyslexic, which her teachers at the time did

CRIME AND PUNISHMENT

not know how to handle, so she did poorly in school and dropped out in ninth grade. As a dropout with a learning disability and parents who did little, if anything, for their children, my mom had hardly any support during her teenage years. The one person who cared for them all was her grandmother, who everyone called Little Granny. Little Granny was a wonderful Christian woman with compassion for everyone. She owned a little greasy spoon diner on the edge of Birmingham, where I would later spend much of my first two years of life.

My mom felt a lot of the responsibility of raising her two sisters even though she was only about a year older. She tried to shield them from some of the problems in their home; most of the time, though, there was no hiding it. She remembers incidents like the police raiding their apartment and threatening both her and Mary. When she dropped out of school, she still wanted her sisters to continue their educations. She would talk as if she were the caregiver of the family, but in reality, it was Little Granny caring for them all. By the time Mom was fifteen, she had already done some experimenting with alcohol and drugs. When she heard about a big party with new tenants in the apartment complex, she was happy to go to the party and get high with my dad, an older boy she had just met. With little support at home, there was nobody to stand in the way when my dad dragged her into the addict lifestyle.

After the big party where my parents met, Dad only lasted a couple of months in that apartment before he got evicted. By that time, he and my mom had gotten serious and Jean liked Dad, so he moved in with them. Dad and Jean went into business together selling marijuana. My grandmother, Jean, would put up the money, my dad would buy and sell it, and they would split the profit. A few months into this business venture, the police raided their operation and found a pound of marijuana. They managed to get excellent lawyers who were able to get Jean off because of a problem with the warrant. The judge reduced Dad's charges to a single misdemeanor, for which he paid a fine. More than that drug raid, which was one of many, what Dad always remembered about this time was it was the last time he played the drums. Dad recalled, "There was a party nearby and the band needed a drummer, so your grandmother Jean took me over there to play. I really loved playing those drums, but the drugs took even that away from me. Addiction was all I had left."

Mom and Dad eventually had a falling out with Jean and moved out. They lived in a hotel for a month,

CRIME AND PUNISHMENT

selling and shooting up heroin like crazy, before they were taken in by Little Granny. Little Granny didn't approve of their lifestyle, but she had so much compassion for them that she wanted to help however she could. After living with Little Granny for a while, Mom and Dad decided to get married. It was 1978. He was twenty and she was sixteen, so they tied the knot at the church Dad had grown up in. After they got married, Little Granny helped them rent a duplex to start their new life together.

As it turned out, their new life looked a lot like their old life, and they continued their hard partying ways. Married life did not have any kind of moderating effect on my dad. If anything, he became wilder and brought my mom along for the ride.

"We were like local legends around there," my mom said. In their corner of the Birmingham area, they were known among the addicts and the police for their crazy antics. Dad loved fast cars almost as much as he loved drugs. "We used to do doughnuts in front of the police station and then outrun the cops," my mom recalled. "Some of them would just go straight to the house instead of chasing us. The only time they really got mad was one time when your dad let me drive. They just couldn't believe this girl outran them."

CHILD OF GRACE: A DEATH ROW STORY

On Christmas Eve of that year, they were partying at the duplex when Dad got in a fight with a friend. The friend left for a minute and then came back in swinging a steel pipe. He broke Dad's arm with it, but it could have been a lot worse since the guy was swinging for Dad's head. God spared him from a more serious or possibly fatal injury. They worked it out the next day. A couple of weeks later, Dad was riding in the car with the same guy when they had a wreck. He broke his arm again inside the cast, but he was so high on Quaaludes and cocaine that he didn't even know it until he went in for a checkup the following week. The doctors performed surgery right away and put in a metal plate and screws. He stayed high in the hospital too. "I had gotten a vial of liquid morphine and got so high I couldn't even see the TV in the hospital room," he told me. When Dad got out, he started writing forged prescriptions. He had grabbed a doctor's prescription pad, and between that and having his arm in a cast, the pharmacies never doubted him. None of his hospital visits even slowed him down in his quest for drugs.

Not long after he got out of the hospital that time, Dad decided to deal drugs to an ex-girlfriend's husband. For some reason, he thought it would be safe to trade this guy a couple of pistols for drugs in

CRIME AND PUNISHMENT

the guy's trailer. It was actually a setup for a robbery, and Dad found himself staring down the barrel of a loaded .44-caliber pistol. He told the guy, "If you blow my brains out, people will hear it all over the trailer park, and you will have a murder charge on your hands." It turned out to be an ironic statement, but in the end, Dad left intact and they even gave him the pills he was there for. The guy who had the gun on him died in a motorcycle crash a few weeks later. The theme of Dad's life continued: he could have easily ended up dead, just like his would-be robber. God still had a plan for my dad.

Soon after this incident, Mom and Dad lost their duplex and had to move back in with Little Granny. It was 1979, and for the first time, Dad actually sought help for his addictions. He realized he had a serious drug problem; unfortunately, he thought the problem was hard drugs and not marijuana or alcohol. He started on methadone treatments, but he soon tired of going to the clinic all the time. He was still selling drugs and smoking marijuana during this time, so he decided he would just kick the heroin habit himself and used some Valium to kill the pain of withdrawals. Dad always said the methadone was harder to kick than the actual drug, and it was just as bad for you. He knew a lot of people who had gotten on the methadone treatment and never got off—they all died of either liver disease or suicide.

My dad's brief spell of being off hard drugs was miraculous in its timing. Since he wasn't shooting up, my mom wasn't either, and since she no longer liked marijuana, the only thing she was doing in early 1980 when she got pregnant with me was smoking cigarettes. By the grace of God, I was spared from what could have been serious effects of maternal drug use. Once they knew she was pregnant, Dad wouldn't let her even think of shooting up, but he had started back doing a little heroin himself. With that kind of drug, a little soon became a lot, and Dad was back to heavy drug usage before I was born. When Mom was four months pregnant, Dad ended up with a warrant out, so they decided to move in with his parents for a while. Leon and Sara and Little Granny tried time and again to help him out of the destructive lifestyle to no avail. They helped him get started in a diesel mechanics course through a government program, but he was shooting up in the bathroom there and you can't very well excel in school while you are doing heroin. Dad even went to church a couple of times with his parents. "I could feel the pull of the Holy Spirit, but I did everything I could to ignore it," he told me. They only stayed with Leon and Sara a

CRIME AND PUNISHMENT

few weeks before they had to move out. They ended up in another duplex right behind Little Granny's diner. Dad managed to stay in school despite being high the entire time and got a telephone sales job to help pay the bills. "I was winning the top sales bonus almost every shift, but I didn't end up with any money because I spent it all on drugs." He was so bad off that Mom was bailing him out of jail while she was going into labor with me.

When I was about three months old, the police raided their duplex again. Shockingly, they did not have any drugs in the house at the time. The police were furious because they knew Dad was a dealer, so they planted a few pills and took them to jail anyway.

"We were standing in the living room and they had searched everywhere, but we just didn't have anything right then. I saw the detective throw some pills behind the couch and say, 'Search behind that couch one more time,' to one of the deputies."

They were able to leave me at Little Granny's diner where I spent most of my time anyway. They got a good lawyer and beat the case, but their lifestyle and the people they associated with didn't change. They left a friend to look after me one night, but he got high on Quaaludes, forgot why he was there, and then left. Little Granny found me some time later and took care of me. Before I was a year old, my parents had separated. Dad had managed to finish the mechanic program and got a job in Birmingham and moved in with another guy he knew. By this time, he had changed his drug of choice to methamphetamines because he was able to function better on that. He and his roommate had several ways to get it, including sending overweight friends to get prescriptions for it as a weight-loss agent and simply forging prescriptions. They had also gotten some lock picks that worked on vending machines; when they got low on cash, they would go steal the money out of some machines. Dad was driving a truck for a different job as well and drove the truck completely wasted most of the time. It was a miracle he didn't kill anybody with that truck. It was also a miracle he didn't kill himself with drugs; even his addict friends were shocked by the massive doses he was shooting. Having a child still wasn't enough to convince Dad to get his life together.

Several months later, Dad got cocky and went to a drug store he had never used before with a forged prescription. This time, he got busted and taken to jail. My granddad let him sit there for seven weeks before bailing him out. Leon thought seven weeks in jail would be enough to dry Dad out and maybe jolt

CRIME AND PUNISHMENT

him out of the lifestyle, but it didn't even slow him down. He went back to the same routine, doing methamphetamines as much as before. My grandmother knew something was wrong because he had the skin-and-bones junkie look and was staying up for days at a time. Once, when he had been on a five-day binge, he decided he probably needed to rest, so naturally, he took a mix of downers to bring him off the speed high. This is the kind of toxic mix that often kills people, and it rendered him catatonic for a while. The girl he was with was too scared to call for help. By the grace of God, he lived, but when he woke up and learned what had happened, it didn't even faze him. Even the overdose death of a close friend didn't convince him to change his ways because he didn't think it could happen to him. "You're so detached from reality on that stuff, and you just think it can't happen to you, like 'I can't die from this stuff' even when you've just seen somebody else die from it."

Shortly after that near-death experience, he went to court for the forged prescription charge. Later, he would realize he could have beaten the case since he wasn't the one to hand the prescription to the pharmacist, but he couldn't afford a lawyer and the court-appointed attorney convinced him to take a plea deal. The plea bargain was for a two-year sentence; he was able to apply for probation rather than go to prison. During the probation, he got caught stealing $77 from a Pepsi machine, so in 1983, he got sent to prison for the first time. He was there for two months before he got out because of a special program for nonviolent offenders. In this program, they would call to make sure Dad was home by ten in the evening and would randomly bring him in for drug tests. It so happened he had taken a bunch of Quaaludes right before one of these drug test calls; he was so high when he got there that they handcuffed him and took him back to prison. This time, he was in prison for a year before they let him out again.

When Dad got out of prison in 1984, he moved in with his sister Nancy and her husband, James, again, just as he had several years before. By then, they had two kids and had settled down a bit. They were struggling financially, so Dad worked with James, who was a painter, for nothing but room and board. Dad was still drinking heavily and smoking marijuana. His parents convinced him to go to church a few times, but he continued to run from God. He would often get high before going. One time, he felt the pull of the Holy Spirit so strongly he had to get up and leave; he didn't go back to church after that. Every time he passed by a church, he would feel a tug on his heart. "I told God, 'I'm gonna get right later, but I'm just having too much fun right now.' In reality, I was miserable, like everyone in that life." A few months later, Nancy and her family decided to move to Georgia. Dad didn't want to move with them, so he moved back in with his parents.

My mom and I had been living with Little Granny, but Little Granny died in 1983 when I was two years old. The way my mom tells it, Little Granny's brother, the executor of her will, had no pity for my mother, and we were literally going to be on the street before my dad's parents took me in. So a little before my third birthday, I moved in with my blue suitcase. I remember having my third birthday party at their house and a few other moments from that time. When Dad moved back home in 1984, I lived under the same roof as my dad for the first time since I was about six months old. I have exactly one memory of my dad from the brief time we both lived there. We were in my grandparents' house playing a game. I would run down the hallway, and Dad would pop out of one of the rooms and grab me. I don't know how long we played that game, but I still remember it clearly. It's the only memory I have of him when he was not wearing a prison uniform. "I don't remember it. I was probably drunk or high," he told me. When he moved in, Leon and Sara agreed to pay for my parents' divorce and then legally adopt me. Dad was still drinking heavily and smoking marijuana, so it wasn't long before he moved out again. I was much older before I understood my grandparents had saved my life by adopting me. God only knows where I might have been without them.

Dad moved in with a friend for a while, but his drinking caused him to get fired from the retail job he had been working since he got out of prison. After that happened, he moved in with my mom and two other women. Dad had been out of prison more than a year and had mostly stayed off hard drugs in that time. After living there for a time, he started doing a little cocaine again. It was like he had never stopped. He went right back to his old ways. Within a few weeks, he had committed two armed robberies. He had even stolen my mom's car for one of those crimes. "Even I was shocked I had done those robberies. I had never committed a violent crime before." He swore he would leave the cocaine alone and never do a crime like that again. Several weeks later, one of the women from the apartment turned him in for

CRIME AND PUNISHMENT

the robberies. My granddad bailed him out, and he promised to go to a treatment program. The program he tried to get into was affiliated with the methadone program he had been in before, and when they realized he still owed them money from 1979, they said they couldn't help him.

Not long after this, a friend of his came upon an almost unlimited supply of pills to sell, and Dad starting selling them and eating them like candy. By then, he had been offered concurrent twenty-year sentences on the robbery charges, his final court date on those charges only a few months away. There was no doubt he was going to prison for a long time, so he decided to raise Cain as much as he could in those last few months. He got arrested several times for driving under the influence, public drunkenness, and other minor things. Dad didn't remember much of this time; he was just running wild. Around Christmas of 1985, he disappeared for over two weeks, from about December 20 to January 5. He never got sober enough in that time to come home, so he missed the holiday season completely. When he did finally show up, he discovered his family had put out a missing person's report on him. My grandparents honestly thought he must have been dead. He had never before been so bad off that he completely missed the holidays with us. I can only imagine what my grandparents were feeling as they went through that holiday season believing their son had probably gotten himself killed. Dad had so many near-death experiences, so many would-be wakeup calls, so many second chances, yet none of them were enough to draw him out of that lifestyle.

Only by the grace of God did he even survive.

I was a teenager by the time I asked my dad about the crime that had landed him on death row. "I guess you're old enough, and you deserve to know," he said. He told me what he remembered. With the final court date for his robbery charges approaching, Dad had continued to do more and more drugs and to get involved with people just as unhinged as he was. People in this lifestyle tend to feed off each other and compel each other into wilder and crazier actions. Dad and some of his friends had met a known homosexual who liked to party in the Center Point area outside Birmingham. The man was a Korean War veteran and was a lot older than Dad and his friends. They had been to his home to party, and the man had paid them thirty-five dollars each to allow him to

CRIME AND PUNISHMENT

perform fellatio on them. Dad and his friends weren't homosexuals, but in the mind of an addict, there was no harm in letting this man perform these acts on them. Thirty-five dollars would buy a decent amount of drugs.

After they had been to the man's home a time or two, they got drunk and high and hatched a plan to commit a burglary. They didn't hate the man or have any particular animosity toward him. They just knew now he had some money and valuables, and they thought it would be an easy score. The three of them struck out on what would be their final crime.

A relative of one of Dad's friends drove the car but otherwise was not part of the crime; later, he would cut a deal and testify against the others. They arrived at the victim's mobile home and discovered he was there. The plan was if he was there, they would get him drunk and then steal from him, but he said he had to be somewhere early the next day and didn't want to get drunk. At that point, the average criminal might have given up on the plan. Terry, the ringleader of this trio, however, was a real macho man and a martial arts expert; he decided there would still be a robbery. Terry, my dad, and a younger man, Todd, knocked the victim to the ground and carried him into the trailer. Terry threatened my dad, and Todd and gave my dad a pocket knife. Terry ordered my dad to get down on the man and stab him in the back with his pocket knife, which he did fifty-nine times. "I don't really remember it clearly. I know Terry threatened us, and I got out my pocket knife and started stabbing him. I got up and said, 'All right, man, let's go now.'" The victim was still alive with these dozens of superficial wounds, so Terry ordered Todd to get a kitchen knife and cut his throat. Todd did as he was told, cutting the man's throat with a kitchen knife, but Terry decided he wasn't doing it right and ultimately finished the murder himself. The three of them brutally murdered a man who had befriended them; they walked away with some appliances and less than one hundred dollars in cash. Dad later said he hardly remembered anything of the crime because he was so drunk. When he awoke the next morning, sober, he thought for a time he had dreamed the whole thing. It didn't take long for him to realize it was no dream; he really had taken part in a heartless murder.

Not long after the crime, children from the neighborhood discovered the victim's mutilated body. It is difficult to imagine how that gruesome discovery traumatized those children. The victim had little known family, so there was nobody left to grieve or later represent him in the courtroom. This man did not deserve this crime in any way; I don't want to leave anyone with the impression that his death was a trivial matter. In no way do I want to minimize his suffering at the hands of my dad and his friends. The victim was loved by God as much as any of us, and I hope with all my heart somehow he cried out to God in his final moments and is in heaven today. Only God knows for sure, but His grace is great enough to save anyone.

A few days later, my dad and the other men were arrested. The driver took a deal in exchange for testifying against the other three who were each charged with capital murder. The three were tried separately, with the same two men prosecuting each trial. A capital murder trial is a lengthy and often sensational event, even in a high-crime city like Birmingham. Dad would be in the county jail for eight months, from the time he was arrested to the time he was sentenced. When he got to jail, he still had some marijuana on him. He smoked some, sold some, and started gambling after being taken to jail to await trial on a capital murder charge. Drugs had him so disconnected from reality that he still did not grasp the seriousness of what he was facing until he had been in jail long enough to sober up.

CHILD OF GRACE: A DEATH ROW STORY

A capital murder trial actually takes place in two phases, with two separate juries, following the US Supreme Court decision in the 1976 *Gregg v. Georgia* case. The first jury only considers guilt or innocence while the second jury considers the sentence, unlike any other trial in which the judge imposes the sentence. The vast majority of criminal convictions in this country are actually the result of plea bargains rather than trials, but with a capital case in which the prosecution wants a death sentence, the defendant always wants to go to trial in hopes of sparing his life. Therefore, all three of the men involved in this heinous crime went to trial.

Dad's memory of the events was hazy, but the three trial transcripts reveal the sordid details of the murder and the events leading up to it. The prosecutors and everyone else involved seemed clear on who was responsible for what and how the sequence of events unfolded. The lead prosecutor said during my dad's trial, "That gutless little wonder [referring to my dad] never would have done it on his own. Terry, the big man, the karate expert, he set it off." The same prosecutor was more emphatic during the sentencing phase: "I try to be honest with the jury . . . And I will tell you today, Terry is the main man. Terry started this whole thing. Terry was the one who cut the victim's throat . . . No, Gary would not have done it on his own. I believed that yesterday, and I believe that today. I doubt if Todd would have." During Todd's trial, the same prosecutor said, "Now I'll tell you this right now. The main man in this operation was Terry. No doubt about it. He was the moving force."

The transcript of Terry's trial was even more telling. The prosecutor said, "Gary Brown got down on that man. Gary Brown put those fifty-nine stab wounds in his back. And you will have a picture of that back there with you. Somebody else did the killing. Recall the doctor's testimony . . . The doctor said, 'Well, none of them penetrated the chest cavity. None was more than two-inches deep. We don't know really how deep the knife went or how long it was because of the compression of the back. But it would be consistent with a two-inch knife.' That's when our man, Terry, Mr. Macho, grabbed him by the head and ripped out his lifeblood. That's what killed him."

In the closing argument, the other prosecutor said, "Terry reached over there and cut the victim's throat right through there. Todd, I submit to you, came over and cut the man's throat, did everything he could. But he was too dumb to know how to do it, according to Terry. 'You couldn't do it right, I had to do it' or 'I had to finish him off,' something like that. And that's what he did. He reached over and cut him like that . . . The victim went down, he died. But up until that final wound, he was alive."

I can only imagine what it must have been like for my grandparents and the parents of the other men to sit through those trials. Terry's mother was close to my grandmother; they remained close throughout the rest of their lives. His mother raised his two children, and I often saw them at church when I was young. I was later told Terry had accepted Jesus Christ as his Lord and Savior, which I pray is true. I was much too young to attend any part of the trial; I don't recall having any idea what was going on at that time. At the end of that year, my granddad retired and we moved from their long-time home just outside Birmingham in Center Point, which my uncle Leonard bought from them, to a house at the edge of the county in the rural outskirts of the Birmingham area. That house in the country was where I grew up.

It is a bit of an oddity in our justice system, what one attorney general would later call a "bizarre result," that three men charged in the same murder can have radically different outcomes. Todd, who had attempted to strike a death blow which may or may not have been successful, served ten years in prison

CRIME AND PUNISHMENT

before being released on parole. Terry was originally sentenced to death but later received a second trial due to a technicality known as a Batson violation. As a result, he received a life sentence he is still serving today. My dad was sentenced to die in the electric chair. By early 1987, when I was six years old, he was on Alabama's death row at Holman Correctional Facility outside Atmore, Alabama. Death row inmates got *Z* numbers—the end of the alphabet for those who would meet their end in that prison.

From then on, he was Gary Brown, Z-472.

CHAPTER 3

Hope in the Darkness

> Train up a child in the way he
> should go: and when he is old,
> he will not depart from it.
> —Proverbs 22:6 (NIV)

The parable of the prodigal son is perhaps the best known of any illustration that Jesus told. Recounted in Luke 15:11–32, Jesus tells the story of a young man who asks for his portion of a father's inheritance, then goes off and squanders every penny with wild living. Starving and humiliated, he finally decides to return home and asks to be a servant in his father's household. We all know how the story ends: the father runs out to meet the son and is so happy at his return that he throws a huge party for him (much to the chagrin of the older brother who never strayed). This parable in particular resonates because of the

HOPE IN THE DARKNESS

grace and love of the father and the idea that we can all be redeemed no matter how far we've strayed. Our heavenly Father is waiting to run to us and embrace us no matter what we've done. Such was the case for my dad as well. Dad took part in a terrible act, the culmination of a long slide into darkness. But God was waiting for Gary, and despite his heinous crime, God granted him salvation and an enduring peace.

When my dad and the others were arrested, it was a major story on the local nightly news. The wife of the senior pastor of my grandparents' church saw it on the news and called the wife of another minister at the church who taught GED classes at the county jail. She called the director of education for the jail and asked if she could meet one-on-one with my dad; he allowed them to meet. She prayed for my dad and, once again, shared Jesus with him. She asked if he would come to her classes and help out. He did so, becoming a great helper and tutor for other inmates at the jail. Once Dad had sobered up, the reality of his situation, the influence of this godly woman, and the memory of all he had heard growing up in church hit him full force. The Holy Spirit used these realizations to bring him to Jesus. Dad found out a couple of his old friends had gotten saved and had been delivered from their lifestyle. He asked my grandmother to bring him a Bible, which she gladly did. One night, in his jail cell, he prayed this prayer: "Jesus, I realize I have completely wasted most of my life so far, and I am oh so tired of running from you. Regardless of what happens from now on, I don't want to run from you any longer. I want to surrender my life to you now. Please set me free from this unbearable burden of guilt and sin." At that moment, he felt the burden lift off of him, like an anvil had been lifted off his chest. "I was in jail, but really, for the first time, I was free," Dad said. He began to study God's Word and commit himself to growing in the Lord. The multitude of prayers for him over all his years of wild living had finally been answered. Ironically, the GED teacher who first reached out to him in the jail was named Mrs. Christmas; she brought the gift of Jesus to my dad. Mr. and Mrs. Christmas would continue to visit him for many years after he was sent to prison.

Holman Correctional Facility is located just outside Atmore, a small town in rural Escambia County, Alabama, about an hour from the city of Mobile, on the Florida state line. There is another state prison located nearby, and before the Poarch Band of Creek Indians built a huge gaming and entertainment center, the Department of Corrections was the largest employer in the county. The department is now a close second and still far bigger than any other employer there. Atmore is also home to a significant Mennonite population. The Mennonites' We Care House, a part of their prison ministry, provided us a place to rest on a number of occasions. Over my many visits to see Dad, a Mennonite family in Atmore would later become as close as family to me. Holman Prison is now less than two miles from the Creek gaming center, but while my dad was there, the prison was not close to anything else, several miles from the town of Atmore.

Dad said when he received the death sentence and was transferred to Holman, he expected death row to be a quiet place with a morbid atmosphere. Instead, it was quite loud, and Dad found most of the guys there got along well and respected each other. The general population in Alabama prisons lives in dormitory-style housing with dozens of guys in bunk beds in one huge room. They were built that way because of a 1960s-era concept that it would aid rehabilitation, but in reality, it is a dangerous and sometimes unsanitary set-up for everyone involved.

CHILD OF GRACE: A DEATH ROW STORY

Death row, on the other hand, is a more typical set of cell blocks, with each of the two hundred or so inmates in a five-by-eight-feet cell with a bed, a sink, and a toilet. Men who could afford it had a TV that got a few local channels out of Mobile; the TV was actually across the hallway from the cell on a shelf and had to be watched through the bars. Contrary to popular belief, they didn't have cable TV. The prison allowed most of the men a radio or boom box to keep in the cell. All but the poorest men also had a small fan in their cell. The prison had no air conditioning, and the temperature easily topped one hundred degrees inside on South Alabama summer days. One Alabama politician, while running for lieutenant governor, later swore he was going to remove cable TV and air conditioning from the prison if elected. This prison had neither, but it certainly sounded good to the tough-on-crime masses.

I don't specifically remember the first time I went with my grandparents to visit Dad at Holman, but I would have been six years old and near the end of my first-grade year in school. My grandparents had put me in preschool at their church when I first came to live with them. Next, they put me in a tiny private school because that school allowed me to start first grade when I was

HOPE IN THE DARKNESS

five years old, which public schools did not allow. After my fourth-grade year, the school closed, and I went to public school.

We visited my dad as often as we could during this time, sometimes making a four-day weekend of it so we could visit him twice in the same trip. Unlike the general population, which had visiting hours on the weekends, death row had visitation on Mondays and Fridays. Visiting hours were eight in the morning to two in the afternoon, so we would wake up at four, stop at a Shoney's along the route for breakfast at six, and get to the prison just in time to start the visit. An inmate could only have one visit per week, so the four-day weekend routine allowed us to visit on Friday, spend Saturday and Sunday on Alabama's gulf coast about an hour further south, and then visit again on Monday. One thing I remember about these trips is we still went to church on Sunday, even while we were at the beach. My grandparents made going to church a priority. They had friends with a small property near the beach, and they would allow us to stay for free during these weekend visits. It was an act of kindness my grandparents truly appreciated. It is amazing how seemingly small actions like going to church on vacation or allowing friends in a difficult situation to use a property for free can have a big impact. God uses even the smallest details and acts of kindness.

○──◆──○

Dad did well during his first few months on death row. At the time, each block had a separate church service, which he attended on Wednesday nights. He was reading the Word every day, praying, and seeking God's will for what was left of his life. He had several offers to purchase drugs that he turned down, but one day, a friend of his handed him a joint already lit and burning, which he took and smoked. It may come as a surprise that even on death row, drugs can get smuggled in, but there are some ingenious inmates and families, as well as some corrections officers willing to make some extra money on something they see as harmless. Dad got high, opening the door for the enemy to derail his life once again.

Accepting Jesus doesn't make any of us perfect; we have an enemy who is real and loves nothing more than to knock us off course. When we are on the right track, we can expect attacks from the enemy. This time, Dad stepped right into it. He smoked marijuana for about a year and even popped pills a few times. He also discovered there was an abundance of pornography available, checking out a book or magazine periodically. He justified the pornography habit by telling himself there were no women in there so it was acceptable to look at some once in a while. He justified the marijuana habit saying he just used it to relax from time to time, which he really needed on death row. After all, marijuana was natural—God made it, so it must be okay.

When a follower of Jesus is doing something wrong, the Holy Spirit lets us know we are off track. We call that feeling conviction. As Dad used marijuana and looked at pornography, the Holy Spirit convicted him. Dad continued to pray and read the Word, and he prayed one of those prayers that the Holy Spirit will gladly answer: "Lord, you know I'm hardheaded, so you may need to knock me in the head to show me some things." One day, he was sitting in his cell smoking marijuana, and he began to think, "Well, since smoking pot is okay with Jesus, then if He were sitting here beside me, do you think He would smoke it too?" Then it hit him: Jesus was there with him because He said He would never leave nor forsake us. Dad threw the joint in the toilet and flushed it. That was June of 1988, and it was the last marijuana he ever smoked.

CHILD OF GRACE: A DEATH ROW STORY

After that, the Holy Spirit began to convict him about pornography. As he got convicted about it, he asked the hall runners not to bring that material to him anymore. He went a little while without looking at any. One day, a hall runner put a pornographic magazine in his door; he picked it up and looked at it. While he was looking at the magazine, his next-cell neighbor, who was a Christian, asked him a question about scripture, so Dad got out his Bible to look it up. The hall runner came back by and saw Dad sitting there with the pornographic magazine open on the bed and the Bible open on his knee and said, "Gary, what you gonna do man, read the Bible or the sex book?" Dad felt awful. He had shared Jesus with this hall runner, and now he had really blown his witness. After that, he distanced himself from the pornography too.

During all this time, Dad went to the Wednesday night church services. The minister who came in to lead them was a good man who meant well, but he often came completely unprepared and would just open up the Bible to read a chapter and make a few points about it. As he was reading some from the Gospel of John, he asked if any of the inmates would like to do a chapter the next week. Dad volunteered and soon began doing it every week. Eventually, the minister quit showing up entirely, but the men kept having church when they were allowed to. Dad went through John and then Acts with the four or five who kept coming. They prayed for some "real" ministers to come in and have church. At the same time, two ministers were praying for God to open a door to work with inmates. The Holy Spirit brought it all together. The prison chaplain brought these ministers in, and eventually, they were allowed to do a single service for all the cell blocks. That was the beginning of Life Row Church. They had services on Mondays, and later, a different group had some services on Thursdays as well.

During the fall of 1989, the men began to be able to take community college courses and GED courses from nearby Jefferson Davis Community College. Dad earned his associate of arts degree a couple of years later, continued taking more courses after he graduated just for the sake of learning more, and eventually ended his studies with a 3.9 GPA. The program was later cancelled when the state decided it was a waste of resources to educate men they were planning to kill. I've always told people I was the first in my family to finish college, but in reality, Dad beat me by a decade.

CHILD OF GRACE: A DEATH ROW STORY

After getting free of some of the hindrances the enemy had put in front of him and the bad choices he had made, Dad did pretty well for a couple of years. He avoided the drugs and pornography and dedicated himself to growing in his walk with the Lord. In 1990, he went back to the county jail for several weeks during a hearing on his case. The appeals process for a capital case is incredibly lengthy and includes numerous hearings and reviews, almost all focused on arcane technical matters of the law rather than culpability or possible innocence. Visiting him at the county jail was a much different experience. There was no long road trip, and it was quite a bit easier to get in and out. Unfortunately, there was no direct contact in these visits. Visiting at the jail is like what is often shown on TV, with thick reinforced glass between visitor and inmate and a phone to talk through. The visiting was not as good in this arrangement, but we took advantage of him being nearby and went several times. Dad stayed at that jail for several weeks but left feeling like he had not been an effective witness for Christ while he was there.

In 1991, Dad got back in touch with a woman he had been into drugs with on the outside. She started to visit him often, and they got to be close. She and the wife of an inmate Dad was close to started riding together to come and visit. In March of 1992, Dad's friend was executed. The woman who had been visiting Dad decided she couldn't take it anymore and quit visiting him. That double whammy had a big negative impact on him. "I was not handling trials in life the way God prescribed. I was mad at God and blamed Him for allowing these things to happen." Through God's grace, Dad continued to lead singing in church, which he had done since 1989, and continued to encourage others. Inside, he was in a spiritual dry spell that would last almost two years. He began to allow the enemy a little space in his life, watching movies and shows he shouldn't have been and placing small bets on a football game here or there. Those may sound like small things, but the enemy will take every chance to manipulate us and get us off course.

Throughout my elementary school years, I was a fairly typical child, although perhaps more academically inclined than some. As typical, that is, as a child can be when being raised by grandparents and visiting his father on death row. My grades were perfect, I participated in all the church activities I was supposed to, and even played church league basketball despite being something less than athletic. My aunt Barbara was like a second mother to me, and my cousins were like brothers. I had extended family that cared for me, including a great-uncle who got me into computers in the 1980s before most people realized how important that knowledge would be. I made a profession of faith and was baptized in my grandparents' church. I also had a relationship with my mom who took me many Sunday afternoons and did fun things like play video games and launch model rockets with me. During those years, she was married to a guy who had a good steady job and seemed completely stable. Later, I would learn from her that he had abused her while they were together, which would be true of all the men she was with after my dad. Life passed somewhat normally and I was a somewhat normal child, but that would begin to change as I approached adolescence.

Throughout my elementary school years, Dad and I would exchange letters, and he would call regularly. I still have a lot of the letters I sent him and that he sent me. I liked to draw pictures and send them to him. Rockets and trains were the most common subjects of my artwork—it seems, even then, I was destined to be some kind of engineer. I would also send him stories I wrote. There were some hilarious ones, like a tall tale about a talking dog. Dad would send me math problems to solve and send back to him; I sent him some homework as well. He always wanted to know what I was doing in school, what I was interested in, and what was on my mind. Dad did what he could to be involved from where he was. As a child I sometimes thought about trying to live at the prison with my dad so I could talk to him any time and play basketball with him on the exercise yard. I didn't understand what I was wishing for; I just wanted to be closer to my dad.

In January 1994, at one of the Monday night church services, Dad was having one of those special times of worship when he could just feel the presence of the Holy Spirit all around him. While he was worshipping, he said, "God, I just want to be one with you. Please let me know if there's anything coming between you and me so I can remove it."

God spoke to him clearly and said, "Gambling." Dad gave that over to the Lord and quit betting on football games. He immediately felt better and went back to his cell feeling good. Then the Lord spoke to him again and said, "What about those movies?" He gave that over to the Lord as well. That was a breakthrough for Dad that got him out of the long spiritual dry spell he had been in. He once again began to really grow in his faith and experience that awesome joy that comes only from the Lord.

Not long before my dad's maternal grandmother passed away in 1981, she famously told my grandmother, "Don't you fret about Gary. He's going to be a preacher." That seemed impossible to believe at the time she said it, but it proved to be truly prophetic. In 1991, God called my dad to preach, but he wasn't totally sure. He talked to the chaplain, and the chaplain advised him to wait until he was positive it was from God. Then came his spiritual dry spell, and he didn't come back to that calling until after his renewal at the beginning of 1994.

Dad helped with some of the logistics of Life Row Church, scheduling an inmate to speak on the first Thursday of each month. As he continued to feel the call to preach, he finally decided he would schedule himself for May 5, 1994. He prayed for God to give him a message, and he prayed it would come quickly and easily so he would know it was from the Lord. That night, God put the entire message into his heart, and he felt confirmation that this call to preach was from the Lord. The following night, he was in a different service when they asked for an inmate to speak a couple of weeks later. Dad volunteered without even thinking about it. He was committed to speak twice in the same week, and as he began to worry, the Lord told him he can give two messages as easily as one. The Lord answered him with another complete message that came to him during his personal Bible study time. Dad committed himself to this new calling to preach, but he hadn't told anybody about it yet. A week later, after one of the Monday night services, one of the ministers came to him and said, "Gary, we need to have you preaching in here." This was the final confirmation that God wanted my dad to preach in the prison; his grandmother's prophetic word came true. God still had much for him to do.

I have tapes of three sermons my dad preached at Life Row Church. One of those tapes is from one of his 1994 sermons; I don't know whether it was the first one he preached or not. The subject of this sermon was loving God. He preached from Second Peter with a lot of Old Testament references added in: "And tonight I'm going to tell you all—I hope this will sink in—obedience is our outward expression of our love for God." He spoke about the importance of serving God for the right reasons: "If there's anyone here tonight that's serving God because they believe He'll get them out of here, you're serving him for the wrong reasons. We need to serve Him because we love Him, because He first loved us. Because He cared enough about us to make a way so we can live eternally with Him." Dad called them to live completely for Jesus: "So what I want to know tonight is are you giving your all for Jesus?" It was a powerful sermon preached by the most unlikely person in the most unlikely place. It strengthens my faith even now to listen to this tape and hear the other men shouting "Amen!" and "Hallelujah!" throughout.

These men on death row were not beyond the reach of God's grace.

CHAPTER 4

The Wrong Direction

> I have suffered much; preserve my life, Lord, according to your word.
> —Psalm 119:107 (NIV)

In late May 1994, there was a huge fight on the exercise yard at Holman. As a result, the warden shut down church and school for seven months to avoid inmates gathering together. In the middle of that time, during the fall of 1994, Dad briefly came back to the county jail for another court hearing. This time, he immediately found a few Christian men who were hungry for the Word of God and led them in Bible study while he was there. The group grew to eight men, one-third of the cell block he was in. Dad taught and preached and felt effective, which made up for some of the feelings of ineffectiveness from the previous stint. Back at Holman, the warden allowed church to resume in December 1994, but he told the chaplain to replace the former minister with new ones. The warden thought the ministers had gotten too close to the inmates, which he considered a bad thing; he didn't understand that, in ministry, developing close relationships is critical to mentoring and making disciples. New ministers did come in, and in 1996, the previous ministers were also allowed to resume their work with the men on death row. Dad continued to get opportunities to preach as well and continued to grow in his ministry from that point forward.

While my dad was overcoming his spiritual dry spell and growing into an evangelist in the prison, I was on a much different trajectory, going full speed in the wrong direction. My first year in public school, fifth grade, went well enough. I got a few disciplinary notes sent home, but nothing major, and the academic part of school was extremely easy because the public school was at least a year behind the my previous little Christian school. Sixth grade was the beginning of middle school, and outwardly, it looked the same—my grades were perfect and I don't recall getting any discipline like the few notes I had gotten before, largely because I learned how to avoid getting

THE WRONG DIRECTION

caught. I wasn't doing anything terrible during this time, just some typical boyhood antics and unwarranted attitude. I did, however, have a growing darkness over me that was fed by the typical changes of adolescence and the circumstances of my life.

In middle school, I was definitely the class nerd, and I was bullied off and on throughout those three years. I never received any serious injury in this era before social media allowed the whole world to share in the torment of the bullied, but I routinely endured verbal bullying and was even pushed down and hit a number of times. During this time, my granddad began to help his sister wind down her business, and for many months, he spent most of the weekdays spending the night at her house about an hour away while helping her. He had understandably suffered from depression during those years, and the work with his sister helped give him something to do as well as a renewed sense of purpose. It also left me with feelings of abandonment. I now realize he was not abandoning me, but at the time, it did not help the growing negative feelings I was experiencing.

As I reached my teenage years, my life began to unravel even more, and the pain and darkness inside me grew stronger. When I was twelve years old, Jean, my grandmother on my mom's side, got back in touch with me. I saw her a few times over the years and spent just a little time with her, but I didn't know her well. Billy, my grandfather on that side, had died when I was seven or eight; he was a drunk almost his entire life and had died from liver disease. Jean had an aneurysm burst in her brain but remarkably survived. She did, however, have some brain damage that affected her ability to speak. Her physical ability to speak was fine and she clearly pronounced words, but her brain was often unable to produce the correct words. A typical example would be mixing up names of related things. One time, she was trying to talk about the Gulf of Mexico, but instead, she said, "We should go to the lake. No, I mean the lake. No. I mean the lake." She knew she had the wrong word, but her brain wouldn't produce the right word, leaving you guessing what she meant. After the aneurysm, she began to call me regularly from her home in Las Vegas. She did this for several months, and eventually, I could understand her pretty well most of the time. I can only assume she felt guilty about not having a relationship with me or her other grandchildren and felt a fresh sense of urgency to do what she could to connect.

Then, one day, not long before my thirteenth birthday, I got a different sort of call from her. "I'm

THE WRONG DIRECTION

going to die," she told me. "I wanted to tell you I'm going to die." I knew exactly what she meant. She intended to take her own life. I told the grandparents I lived with, and they thought I had just misunderstood her or was exaggerating. It so happened that my dad called that night. He thought the same thing—that I had misunderstood her. None of them took it seriously, and a couple of days later, we got word that she had committed suicide. Her role in my life had been nothing more than a strange voice on the other end of the phone, but I was still shaken by the experience. I was particularly traumatized by knowing beforehand and having no one take me seriously. That fed into the swirling feelings of low self-esteem and all the raging emotions that come at the onset of adolescence. I felt helpless, like no one cared, like the world was against me, like nobody understood. It was preteen angst fed by my circumstances, but those feelings were powerful.

My visits with my mother also became much less frequent during those preteen years. She divorced her husband during that time and no longer had the stability of a gainfully employed husband and a house to live in. The last time I saw her as a child was after my thirteenth birthday. I remember talking about her mom's death and how shocked she was, even though they hadn't been close in many years. I got a few phone calls after that and then I heard nothing from her. My grandparents were not upset by this development at all. They had always had nothing but contempt for her and were reluctant to even let her take me on occasion.

Not long before that last visit with her, Mom asked me if I wanted to come live with her. I said yes. I felt pressured by her; it was terribly unfair to ask a twelve-year old that without warning or without any real possibility of it happening. Mom wasn't in any better shape to care for me than she had been ten years earlier, and with my grandparents as my legal adoptive parents, the whole idea was fantasy on her part. Later, I realized even though there was a lot I didn't like about living with my grandparents, I definitely wanted to stay with them. I hated the tension and the potential conflict of having to choose, so I prayed my mom would just go away. I had no idea it would actually happen. I know God didn't send her away due to the prayer of a confused preteen, but at the time, it felt like maybe He had. As time passed without hearing from her, I deeply regretted that prayer and felt a heavy burden of guilt in addition to the loss of the relationship.

THE WRONG DIRECTION

In March 1995, she gave birth to another child, a little girl who would be raised by mom's sister Mary. Mary took the baby and raised her like her own child. It wasn't much later that we saw mom in a segment on the local news called *Crimestoppers*. She had seen the same segment, and she and her boyfriend decided it was time to leave the state. A year or so later, her ex-husband's mother, who was close to my grandmother, called to tell me my mom was dead. She had heard it secondhand that Mom had died in that area. In fact, Mom had actually left the state long before that, but I didn't know it at the time. A few weeks later, my dad heard from an old friend that my mom had been seen at a truck stop in Missouri, which also wasn't true. There were a couple of other sightings before someone had an address. I sent a letter but didn't receive a reply. I spent my teenage years not knowing where my mom was or whether she was even still alive.

I entered high school in the fall of 1994 at the age of thirteen. I was blessed with the opportunity to go to a magnet school, which has consistently been rated one of the top public schools in the nation.

CHILD OF GRACE: A DEATH ROW STORY

This move allowed me to leave the bullying of middle school behind and go to a school full of fellow nerds. I was happy to leave behind most of the people I had known in middle school to go to school with kids who were at least a little bit more like me academically, even if none of them had the kind of crazy family background I did. Even the best public school has problems, and over the course of those four years, easily half of the class drank, smoked marijuana, or was sexually active. Unfortunately, it was some of the more questionable influences who were also the most accepting. A lot of the Christian kids kept me at arm's length. I'm sure they could see I was troubled, and I really can't blame them. At that time, I was reeling from all the things I had experienced in addition to the already powerful emotions of that phase of life. I started to envelop myself in darkness—dark clothes, dark music, dark humor. I decorated my room with black curtains and tried to get my granddad to let me paint the walls black. I had a black windbreaker I infamously wore year-round for a while. It was like an outward symbol of all the negative feelings I had inside, but there was no response to my cries for help. Despite where my dad was, I was emotionally closer to him than anybody else, but even he didn't understand the emotional turmoil I was experiencing. He

THE WRONG DIRECTION

and other family members thought I was being a typical teenager.

I had three cousins with whom I spent a lot of time growing up. My dad's oldest sister, Barbara, had two boys. Ryan was almost exactly my age, and Daniel was four years younger. Dad's other sister, Nancy, had a son two years older than me, Jeffrey, and a daughter who was four years older than me, Lori. We four boys spent a lot of long weekends and summers together, usually at my Aunt Barbara's house. Jeffrey had already introduced us to pornography; he would record it on VHS tapes from premium channels late at night. During my first year of high school, he introduced us to alcohol and hardcore pornography as well. That was the beginning of a pornography addiction I would fight well into adulthood.

The first time I remember drinking alcohol was when I was fourteen. We snuck downstairs at Aunt Barbara's house and each took a shot of vodka from a bottle in the liquor cabinet. Daniel wasn't brought along on these misadventures until he was a few years older. As time went on, Jeffrey was able to get more and more alcohol. I remember a weekend getaway in a cabin at Lake Guntersville State Park when he brought a bottle of Jägermeister that we split. I also had some friends who were able to get alcohol and marijuana during these early teen years. There were a couple of times Jeffrey made plans for us to smoke marijuana together, but for different reasons, it didn't quite work out. Therefore, my first experience with drugs was not with my cousins.

When I was fifteen, my granddad allowed me to go on a class trip to Spain at the beginning of the summer. I'm still surprised he agreed and paid for this trip because, in general, he still carried a Depression-era mindset of never wanting to spend money. I was doing well in school and hadn't messed up as far as he knew, so maybe he was rewarding me for doing better than my dad had or providing an incentive to keep doing well. As it turned out, this trip would be my first experience with heavy drinking and drugs. There were some little hints prior to the trip, but once we got on the airplane, it became clear our chaperones, a husband and wife, were wild partiers who saw no problem partying with teenage students. On the airplane, the husband snatched several miniature liquor bottles and shared them with us. One of the crazier students with us joined the Mile High Club in the airplane lavatory with someone he had just met on the plane.

That trip ended up being a drunken haze for almost everyone involved. The husband bought me a

THE WRONG DIRECTION

bottle of vodka as a gift since I had mentioned trying vodka before. He also scored some Spanish hashish that we all shared and got sky high on. I think the worst offense was when we discovered a group of Spanish girls our age at one hotel we were in. They showed an interest in us, and our chaperone aided us in sneaking up to their rooms for a late-night rendezvous. Mercifully, someone alerted their teacher who rushed in and chased us away before anything happened. A couple of the other guys did end up having hook-ups with girls from other schools in our tour group. We also all went to enjoy the topless beaches of the Mediterranean together. The trip was a nonstop party, and I was stupid enough to think it was a great time despite getting sick and having hangovers. The bigger draw was that these guys were all accepting me just how I was. I remember we were sitting around early in the trip drinking and talking about music, and the husband cut me off and said, "I have an announcement to make: Chris Brown is cool as ——." Literally nobody had ever thought I was cool before. This was the kind of affirmation I had been craving without even realizing it. When we came back from that trip, I had just enough pictures and lucid memories that nobody had reason to suspect I had partied the entire time. Now I regret I didn't get to enjoy the experience of going to Europe for the first time because I spent the whole trip wasted. The only thing that kept me from getting in deeper with that crowd when we got back was the fact that I was still fifteen, and I lived a long way from any of the rest of them.

After I got back, the one person I immediately told about it was my cousin Jeffrey. By that time he, Lori, her husband, and my uncle James all drank and smoked marijuana together periodically. Jeffrey went over to my uncle and said, "Chris got messed up in Spain." Uncle James didn't seem surprised at all. I smoked marijuana with Jeffrey and Lori and her husband several times throughout the rest of that summer. I don't think my other cousins, Ryan and Daniel, ever got into marijuana; at most, they may have tried it once or twice. I had also told one of my best friends, Rob, who I knew from church, and I smoked marijuana with him a few times as well. Sadly, the church youth group at that time was a hotbed of substance abuse and fornication, so there were plenty of others doing the same things we were.

My most foolish moment with marijuana came after school started back that fall. Some of the other drug users who had not been on the trip found out about everything that had gone on. I told one of

THE WRONG DIRECTION

these guys I wanted to get some more marijuana, and I ended up buying a small bag from him in the school bathroom. I still cringe at the absolute stupidity of buying drugs at school. If I had been caught, I would have been expelled and likely would have seen my entire future go up in smoke. Thankfully, God is merciful. He saved me from myself on that day.

I brought that bag of marijuana home in my pocket along with a pipe a friend of Jeffrey's had sold me. The pipe was made from a socket and a sink aerator, so it didn't have to be particularly well hidden because it didn't look like a pipe at all. I unscrewed an old computer joystick I had and hid the bag of marijuana inside the joystick. Only a drug dog could have found it in there. Another trick I pulled during this time was getting a subscription to *Penthouse* magazine. This was during the earliest days of e-commerce, when nothing was particularly secure. I wrote down a credit card number from a Discover card commercial on TV, ordered my subscription online, used a friend's name and my address, and made sure to check the mail at the right time. I got a few issues that way. My granddad got the mail one day and saw the magazine in a black wrapper with my friend's name on it. To his credit, he didn't know what it was. I took it and told him I would pass it on to my friend. The next issue after that came and the package was ripped, so that was the end of that scam. He always believed my friend was the culprit. He promptly called the magazine and had the subscription cancelled. In hindsight, I was lucky nobody got charged with theft. The magazines I hid in the packaging material in a box in my closet. It was not as good a hiding place as the joystick was for the marijuana, but it got the job done. Never underestimate the ingenuity of a teenage boy trying to get pornography. It wasn't much longer before I had a better Internet connection and could find all the pornography I wanted for free.

That bag of marijuana lasted a couple of months because I didn't have a lot of opportunities to smoke it. Living with two retired people meant they were usually around, and not being old enough to drive meant I only got to escape so often. I smoked some of it with my friend Rob from the youth group and some with my cousin Jeffrey; a couple of times, I smoked it by myself. Once, after smoking with Rob, I came home from youth group, and I knew I smelled like smoke because I hadn't had a chance to change shirts. Usually, I would change into a different shirt to avoid the smell and then use eye drops to hide the red eyes. I rushed back to my room and layered on a bunch of deodorant to try and hide the smell.

THE WRONG DIRECTION

Ironically, my granddad hadn't noticed the smoke smell but had noticed the sudden abundance of deodorant smell and asked what I was doing. I was high as a kite and grinned the whole time. I told him some of the guys from youth group were smoking cigarettes, and I had gotten the smell on me. That was actually true; I just left out the part where I left that group and went to smoke marijuana with Rob.

After this encounter, my granddad started saying he was worried about my cholesterol and wanted to get it checked when we went to the doctor for my next checkup. I immediately knew he didn't care one bit about my cholesterol but wanted them to do a drug test on me. So I finished my bag of marijuana by myself, sitting on the back porch of our house on the day before I turned sixteen. I threw out the homemade pipe and didn't smoke marijuana again. My granddad's implicit threat had worked. I feared getting caught more than I wanted to get high. Thankfully, I never tried any harder drugs. I didn't by any means get my life right at that point, though; I just stopped doing what I feared would get me busted.

CHILD OF GRACE: A DEATH ROW STORY

It is hard to overstate how incredibly stupid I was to start drinking and smoking marijuana while my dad was sitting on death row as a living example of where the life of an addict can lead. Along with going the wrong direction with substance abuse, I had also gotten in to some of the darker corners of the Internet and got interested in things like making explosives, which I tried to do a couple of times. One I set off in a neighboring cow pasture, though it hardly did anything. The other my grandad found. I denied it was mine, but he figured out pretty quickly that the matches I had put with it were from our kitchen. That was one of the only times I outright got busted for something. I blamed a pen pal I had met at a summer program for telling me to do it, but it was entirely my idea. I gave up on making explosives because it was hard to do and even harder to get away with. Also, at some point, I realized it was seriously dangerous. I still tried to act like I was into computer hacking and phone phreaking and explosives and all these nefarious things, but all I actually did was read a lot about it. That dark part of me was usually too scared to do anything more than dabble a little bit.

The drinking, marijuana use, and dangerous interests were bad enough, but age fifteen was also

THE WRONG DIRECTION

a low point for me emotionally. I had spent my first couple of teenage years feeling unloved, abandoned, and misunderstood. Most of it was classic teenage angst, but some of it stemmed from the very real things that had happened in my life. In reality, I had grandparents who loved me enough to spend their retirement years raising me, Aunt Barbara who treated me like another son, and Uncle Leonard, my dad's little brother, who also reached out to me as much as he could. Leonard raced motorcycles and took me and my cousins riding pretty often. Later, he would take me out for pizza and let me teach him how to use his computer. My self-centered teen mind couldn't see all of that, and no doubt, the enemy wanted nothing more than to have me spiral into oblivion even as my dad was escaping from darkness.

There were numerous times I just felt overcome with rage or sadness or both. Sometimes I would cry in my room. Sometimes I would wander around in the woods surrounding our property. I still remember the worst episode: I started out just hacking away at my bed with a dull replica sword I had gotten in Spain. That didn't release enough anger, so I went out walking in the woods, ultimately ending up walking almost ten miles to the next town where Rob lived. I called Rob from a pay phone at a little store near his house. Sometimes God watches out for us in the smallest ways. I never carried any change around with me, but for some reason, that time, I had a quarter in my pocket. Rob was already sixteen and had a car, so he picked me up and took me home. By the time he dropped me off, my granddad was outside, my grandparents panicking about where I was. He was mad at first because he thought I had gone off with Rob to do who knows what without telling him I was leaving. He was probably starting to relive the nightmare of things my dad had done. When he realized all I had done was walk a long way, he was still stern, but he just made me sit down and try to explain myself. I spent what seemed like an hour bawling and saying things like "Nobody cares about me" while he just sat there, shell-shocked. At the end of that, he didn't even really do anything. He said something about sometimes forgetting how young I was since I acted mature for my age most of the time. I went back to my room, and nothing else ever came of it. I'm sure he thought it was teenage nonsense, and for the most part it was, but I think I really could have used professional help at that time.

I wouldn't say I was generally or constantly suicidal during this time, but there were some occasions when I had distinct suicidal thoughts. These didn't

THE WRONG DIRECTION

come as a result of any specific thing that happened but were just the result of reflection on my life and all the general dark feelings and emotions I had. There were two times that I came somewhat close to acting on those thoughts. One time, I was in the woods near our property. Deep in the woods was a significant cliff of probably thirty to thirty-five feet. I specifically remember standing there contemplating just jumping head first onto the rocks below. The other time, I had my granddad's small-caliber rifle out. When nobody was home, I used to take it out and fire one or two rounds for fun. He had a couple of boxes of ammunition, so he never noticed one or two missing, especially since my grandmother occasionally asked me to shoot at the squirrels that were destroying her rose bushes. The saddest thing about this is he probably would have loved to go out and shoot with me for fun if I had just told him I was interested. One day, I had the rifle out and loaded while nobody was home. I thought long and hard about putting the barrel in my eye socket and pulling the trigger.

Thank God I literally stepped back from the edge and put the gun down those two times. The enemy wanted to push me over the edge into total destruction and wreak even more havoc on my weary family. The Holy Spirit was there with me, nudging me back toward the light, saving me from myself. God's grace was surrounding me even in my darkest hours. God wasn't done with me either.

CHAPTER 5

Into the Light

> If I rise on the wings of the dawn, if I settle on the far side of the sea, even there your hand will guide me, your right hand will hold me fast.
> —Psalm 139:9–10 (NIV)

When I turned sixteen, things started to get a little better for me. I'm sure leaving the marijuana behind helped. Getting my driver's license and a car also helped. My granddad bought me a car, in part because he was tired of driving me to work and to the school bus stop that was several miles from our house and, in part, as a reward for doing reasonably well in school and mostly staying out of trouble. It was not nearly as nice as that 1968 Mustang my dad was going to get, but I was happy to have it. The car gave me the freedom I was longing for, though I had an early curfew and was not allowed to go to concerts or some of the other events my peers attended. In many ways, I was punished for the things my dad had done; everything they thought might have been part of his pathway to destruction was off-limits for me. My curfew was early, and given how far out we lived, I couldn't even see a movie without breaking curfew. The freedom of my own car also helped me fill the social needs I hadn't been able to before. Living so far from any of my friends was difficult for me as someone who craved social time, so my outlook improved a bit as I was able to better satisfy that need. It also enabled me to go on some dates on my own, which relieved some built-up teenage angst. Luckily, I was a bit of a coward with girls at that age, so nothing unsavory ever happened on those dates. Still, this improvement in my life was not so much a turnaround as it was stepping back from the absolute worst. I particularly regret how bad a son I was to my grandparents and my dad. I completely shut out my grandparents and only had the minimum of communication with them. The people who had given everything for me were now not welcome in the life they had saved. My granddad's depression made it hard to connect when I was young, and all my teen-

INTO THE LIGHT

age emotional problems kept me from connecting as I got older. I also had some pretty nasty exchanges of letters with my dad. "You're just mad because you're in there and can't be out here with me," I wrote in one. He always responded with kindness and compassion, but I was truly mean to him in a couple of letters. He understood me more than anybody else and was far more patient with me than I deserved.

Getting a job was another development that made some things better for me, but it also enabled some other bad behavior. The magnet school I attended had a work-study program on Wednesdays for upperclassmen, so when I started my junior year, I started working at a computer shop not far from the school. I quickly started working in the afternoons on other days and on Saturdays as well. When my sixteenth birthday rolled around that November, my granddad was happy to no longer have to drive across town to take me to work. Working for a little better than minimum wage after school and on Saturdays provided a decent paycheck. I paid for gas and service for my car while my granddad continued to provide the auto insurance.

What might seem unusual is I also paid for my own phone line to be installed in my room as well as for my own Internet service. My grandparents never even knew how to turn on a computer, and with the World Wide Web still in its infancy, they also had no idea what dangers lurked on the Internet. This was long before broadband access was common so I was paying for dial–up service, and having my own phone allowed me to be on it as much as I wanted. Having my own phone line also made for some funny conversations with telemarketers who thought they were talking to an adult homeowner—at least once I ended up telling some roofer to come on out and then watched my granddad tear into him for believing a sixteen-year-old kid was the homeowner. In the earlier days, I had dialed into a couple of the local BBS servers and had direct-dialed friends to play games, but having real web access was something totally different. I could learn about all those dangerous things I was interested in, and naturally, I could find plenty of pornography. It is impossible to overemphasize how deleterious pornography is; that addiction is often more damaging than any substance addiction. The other thing that came along with having a job was I started hanging out with a couple of older coworkers who were quite the partiers. If I spent the night with someone, the early curfew didn't apply. Surprisingly, my grandparents were okay with me saying I was spending the night with people more

INTO THE LIGHT

often than not. I didn't smoke any marijuana or do any other drugs, though one of these coworkers made it clear I could smoke with him, but I did some pretty serious drinking with them on more than one occasion.

Paying for my own phone line also allowed me to receive calls from my dad without anybody else being involved. He could only have eight people on his phone list so I did take up an extra slot, but we both thought it was worth it. My grandmother had no respect for privacy—understandable given the direction some of her children had gone—so she had no shame about listening in on phone calls or opening my mail. My own line solved that problem too. The phone calls from Dad were expensive though, and several times, he asked other family members or friends to send me a check for the cost of a phone call. With the connection charge and the per-minute rate, the calls cost well over a dollar per minute. The calls were also capped at twenty minutes, so even if he could get the phone for longer, he had to call again and I had to pay the outrageous connection fee again. Prison phone systems are notorious price-gougers, enough that some states have had inmates sue and win cases against them. My grandmother couldn't listen in on my phone line, but calls from the prison were monitored. Occasionally, I could hear the telltale clicking that meant somebody was actively monitoring us right then. I'm sure they were bored to death. I had always gotten time to talk to Dad on the phone when I was younger. A regular part of every holiday gathering was waiting for him to call and then passing the phone around to everyone there, which allowed him to catch some people who weren't on his phone list. Having my own line and getting to receive the entire call myself was much better and allowed me to get closer to him. He was there for me and willing to talk about whatever foolishness I had on my mind. Girls and music were two of the most common topics for me, but he worked in something about Jesus every chance he could. He could tell I was struggling emotionally, but even he didn't understand how dark things had gotten inside me or know about the suicidal thoughts. I did eventually tell him I had smoked marijuana but that I had quit, and I don't think he ever told anyone else about it. He just tried to encourage me not to drink and to try listening to some better music, and he always encouraged me to keep going to church and reading the Word.

INTO THE LIGHT

The Sunday after my junior prom was when things really started to turn around for me. After the prom, I had done a little drinking, although I had an early curfew even on prom night and couldn't get into too much trouble before I had to drop my date off and get home. Some of the rest of the group later ended up getting kicked out of the hotel they were partying at because of the underage drinking. They weren't exactly subtle about it and got busted not long after I left. The next morning, I got up and went to church and ended up staying after Sunday school to talk to one of the men who led the class. I told him I had been drinking at the prom, and I had smoked marijuana in the past. He tried to encourage me and told me to call him if I was ever drunk and couldn't get home. It wasn't really a great conversation. In fact, he made some sort of negative comments about my dad that sounded like he doubted the sincerity of Dad's conversion, but the fact that he took time to talk to me and seemed to care had a great impact on me right then. God can use flawed people and flawed conversations to make His grace evident.

Later that day, I was continuing to think and even pray about everything in my life, and I had one of those real and direct experiences with God that felt so tangible it was like He was physically in the room with me. The Holy Spirit enveloped me, and I realized I needed to change, not just in superficial things but deep down in my heart as well.

"Lord, I don't want to be like this," I prayed. "I know my heart has to change, and I can't do it without you. I know you're real, and I need you in my life. Help me, Lord."

And He did help me. My troubled mind seemed to change almost immediately. The darkness that seemed like had swallowed me whole began to fade and disappear. Much of the pain and hate and rage that had been inside me was gone. God's amazing grace washed over me like a wave, and I knew things were going to get better.

I had said the right words and gotten baptized as a young child, but I believe this day as a teenager was when I truly came to know Jesus as my Lord and Savior. I wish I could say my life turned around instantly. In some aspects, it did; I threw out the *Penthouse* magazines and deleted a lot of the dangerous material from my computer. In other areas, it took a long time. Some areas I still struggle with today. With Jesus as my Lord and a real desire to follow Him in my heart, I finally started going in the right direction.

INTO THE LIGHT

I immediately tried to ditch some of the dark and brooding persona I had maintained throughout high school. I also understood for the first time how close I had been to following the same sort of path to destruction that my dad had gone down. I became determined to prove all the doubters and haters wrong. It is surprising how many people, even adults in church, made comments like, "You'll end up just like your dad." One friend asked if it was genetic when she learned where my dad was. I didn't hear this kind of stuff all the time, but it happened on occasion and was extremely hurtful in some cases. Now I wanted to use comments intended to hurt as motivation to do better. I was intent on proving I would not be a failure.

Although I never got close to failing in high school, my grades had slipped some in my sophomore and junior years. I decided I was going to try my best during my senior year; I ended up with a 3.6 GPA in the end, which wasn't bad considering the exceptionally difficult load of classes I had taken. The summer after my junior year ended up being a great one. I was part of a summer scholar program at Birmingham Southern College that allowed me to take two classes there and join other students for a lot of social activities. I continued working at the computer shop and earning some decent money. I also participated in Summer Seminar at the US Naval Academy in Annapolis. I decided I wanted to fly F-18 jets in the Navy and spent much of the next year working through the arduous process of applying to a service academy. I picked my eventual college major while doing introductions at Summer Seminar. They were going around the circle asking what people wanted to major in. I always knew I wanted to go to college, but I was never sure what major I wanted. I was well into high school before I even understood majors and credit hours and how college worked in general. As they were going around the circle, I thought to myself if I wanted to fly jets, I should probably major in something like aerospace engineering, so that's what I said. Eventually, that did end up being my college major. It probably wasn't the most conventional way to pick a major, but it worked out for me in the end.

I started my senior year of high school with a different outlook on life. I still struggled with low self-esteem and definitely made some more alcohol-related mistakes, but I was different. The people around me at school could tell something had changed too. Even the non-Christians said I seemed better. I started spending more time with the "good kids" at school who were now a lot more accepting of me. I had changed jobs to a different computer shop where I continued working for most of the year, though I was laid off in February of my senior year after that shop was bought out. After that, I earned some money working one-on-one to teach elderly gentlemen how to use their computers. When that summer rolled around, I got a job back at the first computer shop I had worked for.

I didn't drink very often that year, but there were a few embarrassing moments. At one party with some friends from the computer shop, I got so completely wasted that I passed out. I couldn't remember several hours of the night when I woke up the next morning half-covered in my own vomit. Apparently, I had said some truly cringe-worthy things to a woman at the party and also tried to throw a punch at my best friend during this time period I didn't remember. Today, I can't understand what people find attractive about getting raging drunk and doing and saying stupid things.

On Valentine's Day of my senior year, I was spending the night at Aunt Barbara's house as I often did, but I had a date that night. My date stood me up, so instead, I ended up with Jeffrey at a party at his brother-in-law's house. I got drunk, and I called Aunt Barbara to ask if I could stay down there. She refused, and instead of admitting I was drunk, I drove a pretty significant distance on the freeway back to her house. I'm sure I was well over the legal blood-alcohol limit. Thank God I didn't get myself or anybody else killed.

During the summer after my senior year, I went on a trip to Seattle with Aunt Barbara's family. They went every year, and I had been there a couple of times before. I knew there was a liquor cabinet in the house we stayed in and my aunt and uncle wouldn't know exactly what was in there when we arrived, so I grabbed a bottle of whiskey and hid it before they had a chance to take inventory. That night, my cousins and I snuck out and went down to the beach with the bottle. Ryan and Daniel drank a little of it, but I drank a whole lot. I can't imagine Barbara didn't know something had happened, but she never said anything about it. Thankfully, these few incidents were all I got into that year, and for the most part, I kept my nose clean and stayed out of trouble. The Holy Spirit continued to convict me and draw me toward the lifestyle God wanted for me.

INTO THE LIGHT

Throughout my senior year, I also continued to work on my dream of flying jets in the Navy. I had earned good enough grades to get in, especially given the highly rated high school I was in. I had scored very well on standardized tests. I had gone through numerous other steps required and gotten past them all. The biggest hurdle is that a nomination from a member of Congress is required for admission. Some of my granddad's friends wrote recommendation letters on my behalf and helped me get to the point of getting interviewed by our US representative's selection panel. I went into the interview room extremely nervous, but I was as honest as I could be with every answer I gave. It turned out they were impressed with me, and I got the nomination. I still have the nomination letter, with a handwritten note from the congressman on the back telling me how impressed the selection panel was. I had a high school friend who had gotten interested after I came back from Summer Seminar and told him about it, and he got the other nomination from that congressman. In addition to getting my grades up, I had also spent the year trying to get in physical shape, going from a scrawny 135 pounds to a respectable 155 pounds that year. My classmate and I were all prepared for our future in the Navy and were waiting on our official appointment letters in the spring of our senior year. I had been required to apply for a waiver after my physical exam due to my eyesight, which was a commonly granted waiver.

What happened next came out of left field. I received a medical disqualification for minor depression. During my exam, I had marked on the form that I had sleepwalked when I was younger. The doctor asked about my family and any potential traumas in my life, so I told him the truth about my whole family background. He had asked if I ever felt depressed. I said once in a while I felt down just like anybody, and he had replied, "I'd be down sometimes too with all that in my life." I didn't think anything of it at the time, but the system said I had minor depression. These rulings could be appealed, which I did, but that process moves so slowly that I had no hope of getting an appointment to the academy for that year. I did see a psychologist for an assessment who agreed I did not have any issues that should preclude my serving, but by then, it was way too late. To this day, I joke that I have an official letter saying I'm not crazy, and my wife jokes I was the only one who needed a letter to prove it.

During college, I became friends with a professor who had been a commander in the Navy. After

INTO THE LIGHT

hearing my story, he believed my family history was the real reason they disqualified me, and they didn't want to take a chance on me. I didn't believe him then, but with age, I realized he was probably right. When the news of the disqualification came, I was surprisingly at peace about it. God gave me complete serenity about the situation. This was one of those times that God, in His wisdom and grace redirected me, even if I didn't totally see that at the time. I know now I was much better off on the path I took. I don't know whether I would have been successful at the academy, but I know I would be a different person with a very different life if I had gone there. My classmate who got a nomination not only got to fly F-18s but flew with the Blue Angels; he was truly living that dream. I wouldn't trade with him for anything in the world.

The biggest immediate problem after my sudden disqualification was I didn't really have a back-up plan. What I had claimed was my back-up plan was too expensive for me, and even with great test scores, I couldn't get enough of a scholarship to make it work. Because of my good test scores, I had a mountain of literature from hundreds of colleges around the country that I had just stacked in my closet. I was about to graduate, I was well past the nominal application date for any of these schools, and there I was sifting through mailers seeing if anything stood out. All I knew was I had to go to college, and I wanted desperately to get out of the house and get out of Birmingham. I also had that idea of majoring in aerospace engineering that I had decided on spontaneously almost a year earlier.

That's when I saw the material from the University of Alabama in Huntsville (UAH). The Holy Spirit told me as soon as I saw it that was where I would go to college. He didn't tell me I would eventually earn four degrees there because I probably wouldn't have believed Him. It was one of the few moments in my life that I clearly and directly knew what I was being led to do. Despite being less than two hours away, I didn't know the first thing about UAH. I didn't have the opportunity to go to Space Camp in Huntsville like so many of my classmates had. I discovered there was a great little tier-1 national university with a fantastic engineering school that had grown up along with the space program in Huntsville, right there in the northern part of my state. All this, and it was a public school with

INTO THE LIGHT

affordable in-state tuition. I applied, was accepted, and, even though I had applied months after the scholarship deadline, still received two scholarships. In a matter of a few weeks, I went from service academy disqualification with no idea what to do next to having a clear path forward. God's grace was certainly covering me during that time.

Everything else about my senior year went pretty smoothly. I had all the typical experiences at senior prom and graduation. I took the toughest possible course load and still did well. I participated in some extracurricular activities like Science Olympiad, where I won medals at the district and state levels. But, most importantly, despite my setbacks and mistakes, I had started to grow in my faith and walk with the Lord more and more. I was still pretty cynical, but most of the darkness had left my mood and personality. I no longer had suicidal thoughts. I still struggled with self-esteem but not in the same way I had previously. I still didn't allow for a great relationship with my grandparents, but it did improve as I got better. The summer after my senior year was another good one despite the chaos of figuring out college plans at the last minute. Seeing I would soon be out on my own, my grandparents loosened up a lot on their rules about curfew and what sorts of things I could do.

After years of darkness, I had finally stepped into the light. I was ready to see where God would take me next.

My dad was a big part of my life during this time and helped guide me in the right direction. He had been on the board of a prison-based abolitionist group called Project Hope for many years, and we worked on a newsletter called *A Christian Perspective* together. He continued to lead worship in Life Row Church and got to preach from time to time. He also led a number of people to Christ, both in and out of prison. Our little newsletter even started at least one person on the path to salvation. God can use the most unlikely things and the most unlikely people for the work of His kingdom.

I have another tape of Dad preaching from this time period. He had preached many times since that first sermon in 1994 and was great at sharing the Word of God. The theme of the sermon from the late 1990s was "Be Strong and Courageous." Starting in First Chronicles chapter 19, he exhorted the men

INTO THE LIGHT

to have the strength to truly live for Jesus: "So it takes strength to live for Jesus, and by that I'm talking about sold-out living for Jesus. I'm not talking about cussing with the sinners and praising with the Christians, telling a dirty joke over here and talking about God over there. I'm talking about living for God, every minute of every day what He wants us to do." He encouraged them to look to God rather than their environment: "Guys, if we start looking at our circumstances tonight instead of looking at the power of God, we're gonna fall weak just like them. We can't look at our circumstances. Circumstances will fool you. Satan can set up circumstances. God can overcome circumstances. He tells us to be anxious for nothing. He tells us today's got enough troubles, don't worry about tomorrow. Seek first the Kingdom, all else will be given to you." He admonished them not to compromise: "Do not turn from it to the right or the left, no compromise. No taking the eyes off Jesus and looking on the circumstance. Then you can be strong and courageous." Lastly, he made sure they knew claiming to be Christian while living like the world was a serious problem: "Fellas, I'm gonna tell you tonight, it's not a light thing to blaspheme God. But the name of God has been blasphemed if you profess the name of Jesus and you don't live like you know Jesus." It was another powerful message that resonated at Life Row Church then and still resonates with me today.

CHAPTER 6

Ain't Got Time to Die

> And they overcame him by
> the blood of the Lamb, and
> by the word of their testi-
> mony; and they loved not
> their lives unto the death.
> —Revelations 12:11 (KJV)

I started college at UAH in the fall of 1998 at the age of seventeen. By the grace of God, I was on my way to being the first in my family to attend university and complete a degree. I started out with my declared major of aerospace engineering, which at the time was technically mechanical engineering with an aerospace concentration. By my second year, I had decided to add a second concurrent degree program in astrophysics. I'm still not sure exactly why I added the second degree program; it just sort of seemed like something I wanted to do. I had earned a lot of advanced placement credit in high school and had two classes from the summer program I had attended the year before, so I started college just two credit hours short of being a sophomore. By the end of my first year, I was a junior in credit hours. It would still take me five years to complete the two degrees, partly because of the number of classes I needed but mostly due to my own self-inflicted problems. Like a lot of kids who move away to college, I immediately got swept up in social activities and extracurricular clubs. None of these things were inherently bad, but I would spend a lot more time on them than I did on my actual coursework with predictable effects. A lot of people who know I got two highly technical undergraduate degrees (and later two graduate degrees) just assume I was a fantastic student, but I was actually a poor student through most of my undergraduate years and barely crossed the finish line at the end with a disappointing GPA. The last couple of years after I had met Sarah, the woman I would later marry, she dragged me along in part by helping me study and in part by providing motivation that I didn't want her to graduate before me since she started two years later. I could blame the tough events in my life or the fact that I worked almost full-time most of those years to pay my bills, but in truth, I could have been a better student if I had focused on my coursework and kept my priorities in order. Instead, my coursework was often last on my priority list and the first thing to get dropped when life got too busy.

I started college with two scholarships, a prepaid tuition program my granddad had invested in that covered most of my tuition costs, and a little bit of money saved from my high school job. I was in pretty good shape, but I still got an on-campus job that stemmed from one of my extracurricular activities. By happenstance, I went to a fraternity party my first weekend on campus, and a guy there asked if I was interested in space. Being a good nerd in the Rocket City, I said yes, and he introduced me to a club that was building a satellite. In October of 1998, it became the first ever student-built satellite launched into orbit, beating the likes of the Navy Postgraduate School and Stanford University that would later launch their own satellites. I got to work on it as a brand-new freshman and then had a paid job operating the ground station for it. I don't believe in luck, and I know I didn't do anything to be qualified to take part in that, which can only mean the Holy Spirit dropped that opportunity right in my lap.

CHILD OF GRACE: A DEATH ROW STORY

I had a lot of other incredible experiences at UAH, like flying on NASA's microgravity simulation aircraft and travelling to conferences all over the country. These were all good things, but along with my ever-present social needs and my belief that I needed a job, they all drew attention away from my studies. Most of my undergraduate years, I worked a combination of on-campus jobs and computer repair jobs, often with paychecks coming from three different sources. One of my scholarships was only good for one year, and in my second year of college, I lost the other one because my GPA was below the limit. Several times. I started a class and then dropped it after the refund date, which squandered some of the prepaid credits my granddad had invested in. Between squandering some credits that way and the fact that my two degree programs required far more credits than were in the prepaid program, I ended up paying a lot of my own tuition by the end. I did get another one-time scholarship near the end of college, not so much because I deserved it but because I got a hot tip that only one person had applied. They had two scholarships to give out. I got one, and Sarah got the other one. I was also blessed to get my first real engineering job at the age of nineteen. That turned into a full-time job that paid well, enabling me to buy the house I still live in today.

That was another Holy Spirit moment, both the idea to buy the house and being led right to the perfect house for me. It was the first one I saw; I only looked at others because it seemed foolish to just buy the first house I ever saw. I rented rooms to three roommates who effectively paid the mortgage with their rent and split all the utilities. This arrangement brought my cost of living down pretty low. That was a blessing because I got laid off after the September 11 terrorist attacks caused budget realignments and contract cuts. I went back to my hodge-podge of on-campus jobs and computer repair jobs, and with my low cost of living, I was able to scrape by for the rest of my undergraduate years, albeit with help from my grandmother a couple of times.

I wish I could say my inability to prioritize as a student was my only real mistake in college, since I was now growing in my faith and trying to serve the Lord. Like my dad and almost anyone else, I still made plenty of mistakes along the way, most of them involving girls. I drank a few more times, though never enough to get wasted, before I finally quit at age nineteen. I don't believe the Bible says a Christian can't drink alcohol—Jesus turned water into wine, after all—but with my family history of alcoholism and some of my own experiences, I knew I didn't need it in my life.

Before I met Sarah, I had a string of toxic relationships. One was a long on-again, off-again affair that was detrimental for both of us, and a few more were short-lived mistakes with girls I never should have gotten involved with. These mistakes were all run-of-the-mill college imprudence, regrettable as they were, but I know now my biggest problem was pride. It may sound paradoxical that someone could struggle with low self-esteem and foolish pride at the same time, but I believe it is quite common. It was my pride that made me think I could somehow maintain an arm's-length list of extracurricular activities, a job or two or three, and a full class load. It was foolish pride that made me think I could do well in classes even if I skipped a lot of them. And, most of all, it was that foolish pride that made me think I had to work full-time and support myself. I wanted to get away from home and on my own so badly that I took classes and worked every summer. I felt like I had to do it all myself because I was too proud or too scared to ask my granddad for financial help. In hindsight, I know he would have supported me financially as long as I was in school and passing my classes. Pride can be the most insidious and destructive sin we deal with, and it made my life far more difficult than it needed to be.

In the fall of 1999, I was at home for Thanksgiving when the phone rang late at night—before midnight but much later than anyone would be calling my grandparents.

A male voice on the other end said, "Is this Chris?" After I said yes, he said, "Is this line clear?" I said yes again. After all, my grandparents were asleep, and I couldn't hear anyone moving. Then he said, "I have someone here who wants to talk to you."

It was my mom.

For the first time in years, I was hearing from my mom. She was alive, staying in Birmingham at her husband's parents' house. Even though it was late, I agreed to go to their house in downtown Birmingham right then. When I opened my bedroom door, my grandmother was standing there. She had listened in on that conversation because she still had no shame about invading my privacy. She tried to give me a curfew, but I rejected that in no uncertain terms. I said I would be back when I got back.

She said it was up to me to tell my granddad I was back in touch with my mom. I never did tell him, and I don't think she did either.

I drove over to the home of Mom's husband's parents. She called him her husband, but they were never legally married. It turned out his parents were both university professors; in fact, his whole family were really wonderful people. In their living room, I saw Mom for the first time in years. My first question was simple: "Where have you been?" She had been consorting with all the wrong people, evidently, and when she got pregnant with my half sister, she had nowhere to stay. Mom didn't do any drugs then, evidenced by the fact that my half sister was a healthy eight-pound baby, but she stayed at a local crack house. Her aunt had stolen Mom's checkbook and written a bunch of bad checks; that aunt did something similar to another relative as well. When my half sister was born, Mom was in trouble due to where she had been staying and due to her aunt's misdeeds. Her sister Mary came and took custody of the baby. That's when Mom saw herself on the news and decided to leave. They went first to Florida where they got in some trouble and lost a vehicle. Then they went to Louisiana on a tip that there were plenty of jobs there. That tip was out of date, and instead, they ended up spending a few years living in a drug haven of a trailer park. They moved and got clean and, on this risky visit back to his parents' house, decided it was time to make contact with me.

After that midnight visit, we decided to have a family reunion of sorts at Aunt Mary's house the next day. That reunion would be the only time my mom, my half sister, and I were together. I had visited my half sister at Aunt Mary's often since she was a baby and continued to go see my half sister after I went to college. Mom pretended to be her aunt to avoid upsetting her belief that Mary was actually her mother. I still have a stack of pictures from this reunion. For one day, that part of the family seemed a little bit normal. That would be the last time I would see my half sister in person until a chance reunion almost twenty years later. The next couple of times I stopped by, I was told she wasn't there or was at someone else's house. In reality, that family had started to come apart. Within a few years, the dad of the family, Uncle Charles, would die by overdosing on a combination of methadone and alcohol. Mary would end up in a shelter and later an institution before she died at the age of forty-eight, the same age that her mother died. She had two boys a little younger than me who were left mostly on their own. My half sister, it turned out, had been sent to live with another family that we didn't know anything about.

We would spend many years trying to track my half sister down. I've now gotten in contact with her and my cousins from that part of the family through social media. I still hope we all can have a real relationship one day. Mom would later have another girl more than twenty years younger than me with a different man after she split from her husband. That daughter was taken from her in a particularly cruel way with the help of some corrupt local officials. The loss of those two girls led her into life-long depression and alcoholism. My relationship with Mom was always a struggle. It was my wife who later helped me see we did not have an appropriate parent-child relationship, and I shouldn't have to do things like call the sheriff to check on warrants or drive to Louisiana in a hurricane to help her at a court hearing. Later on, Mom would get in trouble a couple more times and spend a little time in the local jail before getting off drugs for good. We continue to visit her occasionally and talk on the phone sometimes. She has had some involvement with a local church that helped do work on her home, and she says she is a Christian.

I continue to pray she comes to fully walk in God's grace.

○━━◆━━○

Around the same time I reconnected with my mom, in the late fall of 1999, my granddad got sick. His forty-year career in the coal industry and his rheumatoid arthritis had led him to have a condition called pulmonary fibrosis. By early 2000, he was on an oxygen tank. I was away at college and was not diligent about staying in touch, so I had no idea how serious his condition was in the spring of 2000. The rest of the family was not keeping that information from me, but nobody went out of their way to keep me informed either. As Easter was late that year, on April 23, and I had finals coming up and a lot of other things I thought were important going on, I decided not to go home for the holiday. I ended up with deep regrets over that choice. Later that week, I got a call that he was in the hospital, and I should come visit. Even then, I didn't realize how serious his condition was, so I had made plans to see an old friend while I was in Birmingham for the weekend. When I got to the hospital, the mood was much more somber than I expected. On the Saturday after Easter, I went in to see him for the last time as he lay in a hospital bed. I just stood there speechless.

"I know it's shocking," he said.

My grandmother and Aunt Nancy were in the room, and somehow, with them there, all the things I wanted to say to my granddad just didn't come out. I went to the bed, hugged my granddad, and told him I loved him. I had so much more than that to say, but the words weren't there. He went to be with the Lord in the early morning hours of Sunday, April 30, 2000, one week after Easter Sunday.

I stayed at home as the funeral arrangements were made and ended up having to postpone one of my finals. I took the final for a particularly brutal physics class two weeks later and narrowly managed to pass the course. Along with the typical funeral arrangements, we also worked to see if there was any way my dad could come. It was a long shot, but another death row inmate had recently been allowed to attempt to help his ailing father as a donor so there was some possibility it could happen. Our family was close to a local sheriff's deputy, and he had offered to drive and do escort duty on his own time. We delayed the funeral arrangements a day as we made our effort, but the warden denied it. He would have a real problem on his hands if every inmate asked for a pass every time a loved one died. We decided it was for the best because the sight of my dad in prison whites and shackles in the back of the room likely would have disturbed everyone there. In the end, it was a typical funeral, although one in which there was not nearly enough room for everyone who came.

I was nineteen years old when my granddad passed. This man had given up a lot to rescue me, and he had done his best to be a father to me. His struggles and mine often made that difficult; I spent all of my teenage years pushing him as far away as I could. At nineteen, I had just started to appreciate him the way I should have all along, and I had just started to make the first overtures toward a better relationship with him. I regret I didn't get to tell him how much he meant to me in this life, but I hope he would be proud of me now. Many years later, I would learn he did not receive all the honors he should have from his military service, so I worked to have the Bronze Star Medal posthumously awarded to him. We had a big ceremony at my workplace with the congressman who aided the case and a two-star general who championed the ceremony. My granddad's younger brother and only surviving sibling, also an Army veteran, received the medal on his behalf. Working to get that medal awarded and have a ceremony in his honor was one way I felt like I could show my granddad some of the respect he should have gotten from me while he was alive. It brought a measure of closure for me. He was a great man. I know I will see him again in heaven.

○──◆──○

During this time, my dad continued to correspond with me regularly and call when it was possible. I visited when I could, but there were limitations like the age restriction on visitors and my college schedule that made the visits harder to arrange than when I was younger. Our conversations had turned more toward my interests and my growing faith. Dad sent me Bible study material along with a lot of articles and notes on scientific topics and sometimes on politics. I had continued to work on the *A Christian Perspective* newsletter with him and started the first version of the group's website. Particularly during this period, Dad got me interested in Christian apologetics, the factual evidence and rational proofs of the Christian faith. He sent me articles from several famous Christian apologists and got me copies of classic books like Josh McDowell's *More Than a Carpenter*. This all bolstered my faith as I studied in secular technical fields and also birthed a lifelong interest in studying apologetics.

By the time I entered college, Dad had been on death row more than eleven years. The appeals process is lengthy, but it is not infinite: we knew eventually the attorney general's office would request an execution date, which would be granted by the state Supreme Court. In early 2002, this time finally came, his execution date set for April 2002. At this point, the regular appeals process has been exhausted, and only two possibilities for a reprieve remained: clemency granted by the governor or a stay of execution issued by the United States Supreme Court. Both of these were long shots. We hoped the disparity in outcomes of the three cases, along with Dad's clear and convincing rehabilitation, would sway the governor to spare his life. At the same time, Alabama was one of only two states still using the electric chair, and we also had hope the US Supreme Court would issue a stay based on the eighth amendment to the US Constitution.

The governor receives clemency petitions through his chief counsel. The chief counsel at this time was personally against the death penalty, serving under the last of the old-fashioned conservative Democrat governors to lead Alabama. The governor had been attorney general earlier in his career and was undoubtedly in favor of the death penalty. As the chief counsel received information for the clemency petition, it was clear he was moved by the case. There was no hearing for clemency; the petition was just made through this man. He was so moved he went and visited my dad at Holman Correctional Facility. That experience convinced him my dad was a changed man whose execution would serve no positive purpose. We felt like perhaps we had a friend at the capitol.

When the week of the execution date came, Dad was moved to the death cell, a special cell near the execution chamber where the condemned are watched around the clock. The prison ensures the inmate does not commit suicide before he is executed. The governor at that time had always made his clemency decision, which had always been a denial, on the Monday of the execution week. Monday came and went with no decision. We took this as a good sign that, maybe if nothing else happened, the governor would grant clemency. Politically, it was better for him if he didn't, so we assumed he was waiting for a possible Supreme Court stay before acting himself. The execution would take place one minute after midnight on Friday, so Thursday was the final day of visiting with my dad. That morning, I had gone to the state capitol to make one final plea to the governor. I didn't see the governor, but I did see the chief counsel who assured me the governor had carefully reviewed the petition. That afternoon, we visited with my dad. It was just us in the large visiting yard, so eerie with nobody else present. Dad's best friend, John, had come from out of state, a local Mennonite pastor acting as his spiritual adviser was with us, and, of course, family members came and went. We talked about all sorts of things, times we remembered together, things that happened in the past, and, most of all, about God's grace. We sang some hymns and old spirituals. John was a gifted musician and the minister of music at his church; he had recently recorded an album of old spirituals. There was one in particular Dad wanted us to sing called "Ain't Got Time to Die."

We finished singing songs and talked for a while before John, his spiritual advisor, and I decided to go get dinner. We had to eat and get back before they closed the gate to the prison and would not allow us back in for our final few hours of visiting. We went to the Golden Corral in Atmore, one of the few restaurants in town. While we were sitting there at dinner, the call came in: the US Supreme Court had issued a stay of execution. The stay came in about eight hours before he was scheduled to die. It turned out at the exact moment we were singing "Ain't Got Time to Die," the court was making their ruling for a stay. Dad didn't have time to die that day; God still had more for him to do. Only God could orchestrate that incredible moment.

CHAPTER 7

Politics Become Personal

> That is why I am suffering
> as I am. Yet this is no cause
> for shame, because I know
> whom I have believed, and am
> convinced that he is able to
> guard what I have entrusted
> to him until that day.
> —2 Timothy 1:12 (NIV)

I had peace during the entire time period leading up to Dad's first execution date. I believe the Holy Spirit was letting me know Dad's time on the earth wasn't done yet. There was really no time leading up to his stay of execution, only eight hours prior to his scheduled time to die, that I felt like it was actually going to happen. God is good, and in His grace, He granted me peace and comfort throughout that time.

CHILD OF GRACE: A DEATH ROW STORY

After the news of the stay came in, we were not able to go back to the prison for any more time with Dad. With his impending execution on hold, we no longer got the special visitation time. I made the long drive back to Huntsville and wrapped up my penultimate year of college. I had asked a lot of my friends to write letters to the governor asking he grant clemency. It's hard to know what impact that sort of thing has, but staff members have indicated they do look at all the letters that come in and often recorded how many people call or write for or against clemency. It's hard to imagine the staff sitting around tallying letters to determine whether the masses want someone to live or die. Naturally, everyone was relieved about the stay, and we were happy to at least have more time with Dad. By this time, my grandmother had moved out of the house I grew up in and into a much smaller home she could easily maintain. The family went on with life as usual almost as if nothing had happened. Perhaps none of us really believed Dad was going to die that time. Perhaps we were starting to believe he really might not die at the hands of the state after all. There had been some prophecies about freedom and some legal details that made it seem possible, leaving Dad really believing these prophecies meant earthly freedom.

POLITICS BECOME PERSONAL

Leading up to that execution date, I had some of my first direct experiences with the press. About two years earlier, I had been interviewed by a reporter who was doing profiles on certain death row inmates. She was very pleasant and easy to talk to, but when Dad learned each of her stories led with all the gruesome details of the crime, he nixed the whole thing. During that time, he was also told his case might be featured on *60 Minutes*; in the end, they found another case that was more interesting. Only God knows whether that press exposure would have been good or bad for us. The most appalling thing that happened during this time, however, was when a local news camera crew showed up to my grandmother's church one night during the week of the scheduled execution. I'm sure it was easy for them to discover where she went to church, and they were able to determine she would probably be there that night. Fortunately, she was inside in the nursery area, where she often volunteered, when the crew arrived, and some of the men from the church were able to compel them to leave the property. We were shocked and outraged that a so-called journalist would seek out a widow whose son was about to be executed at her place of worship.

CHILD OF GRACE: A DEATH ROW STORY

Gubernatorial elections in Alabama happen on the midterm years of the federal election cycle, so 2002 was an election year. No doubt that was why the sitting governor, who was running for reelection, had not said anything about clemency; if he really intended to grant clemency, he was going to wait as long as possible and see if something else took care of the situation. That governor lost the election and was the last of the old dominant Democratic Party to serve as governor. The new governor was only the second Republican to serve as governor since Reconstruction. With a new governor under a different party, an entirely new staff occupied the state house after he took office in January of 2003. The new governor and the new staff would also have a different process for considering clemency petitions. In Alabama, the governor's authority to grant clemency does not come with any particular set of rules, and each governor has a lot of freedom in how they choose to accept and consider petitions. By the beginning of 2003, Alabama had followed most of the nation in adopting lethal injection as a method of execution. This change removed the stay of execution that had been granted based on use of the electric chair; the first execution by lethal injection in the state took place on March 13, 2003. The new governor had pledged he would witness the execution as a show of taking responsibility and no doubt to sound tough on crime, but in the end, he wasn't there.

Everyone believed after the fact that Dad's original lawyer had been subpar. When the appeals process began, the family hired a new lawyer. I remember him coming to my grandparents' house to meet with them when I was young. I snuck down the hallway and listened in on the meeting. The details weren't terribly memorable, except that they paid a large one-time fee and were told they would not be charged any more after that throughout the process. By the time of the first clemency petition for the first execution date, Dad had switched lawyers again. Technically, the lawyer my grandparents had hired for the appeals was still active, but Dad had switched his primary counsel to a pro bono lawyer from the nonprofit Southern Poverty Law Center (SPLC). The SPLC is a liberal organization that has drawn the ire of many Christians by erroneously listing some Christian organizations as hate groups. Nonetheless, they also do a tremendous amount of good work combating real hate groups, helping indigent defendants, and working on cases in which clear injustice has taken place. The SPLC lawyer who worked on Dad's case was excellent and did everything she could to help us, down to paying for a hotel room in Montgomery when I tried to see the governor. She would be the one to file the clemency petition for the original execution date, and she filed the petition for the new governor after the attorney general's office had requested and received a new execution date of April 24, 2003.

This time, the governor's chief counsel scheduled a clemency hearing at the state capitol in Montgomery. It was unclear to me whether the previous execution had been preceded by a clemency hearing. If it had been, nobody in our group was privy to the details, or at least hadn't shared them with me, so I really didn't know what to expect. Would the governor be there? Or would he only be represented by his chief counsel? Would anyone from the attorney general's office be there? I had in mind that the hearing was basically a matter of us begging for mercy, and I naively thought the governor would hear our petition himself.

The written petition, a full half-inch thick with numerous letters and excerpts from the trial transcripts, began with a list of who would attend on my dad's behalf: several family members, Dad's best friend John, a former chaplain at Holman, a former assistant chaplain at Holman who travelled from

POLITICS BECOME PERSONAL

out of state, the former pastor of my grandparents' church, the minister who led the church on death row, and Dad's old friend and former minister Mr. Christmas. The two chaplains had never before spoken on behalf of a condemned inmate. The chaplain serving at the time also wrote in support of clemency and several corrections officers volunteered to be references, both of which were unprecedented. The petition had seven sections following the two arguments for clemency, namely that Dad was completely reformed and he was least culpable in the crime yet he was the only one facing a death sentence. The first section was Dad's own statement. The second section was a set of letters from the chaplain at Holman, family members including myself, and a number of prominent ministers in the state who knew my dad.

The next section had perhaps the most surprising letter: an investigator from the sheriff's office who worked that case and to whom my Dad ultimately confessed. Like almost everyone else who wrote, he was not opposed to the death penalty, but he believed it was unjust in this case. Following that was a section about the many clemency requests that had been granted around the country; only one was from Alabama, a woman infamously granted clemency in the final days of a former governor, who gave no reason for his decision. The fifth section included numerous excerpts from the trial transcripts that demonstrated even the original prosecutors at the time knew my dad was the least culpable of the three killers.

The following section was also a surprise: four of the original jurors who had voted for a death sentence wrote to ask that Dad's life be spared. They had realized the outcome was unjust.

The final section had Dad's degree from Jefferson Davis Community College, his transcripts, and some certificates from various Bible courses he had completed via correspondence. It was a hefty and convincing volume of material. With unprecedented support, no living family or friends of the victim to object, indisputable evidence of reform, indisputable evidence of lesser culpability, and a governor who would not face an election for more than three years, I thought we had the best argument for clemency that could possibly be brought. Even the former governor's chief counsel, who was so moved after his visit with Dad, offered to help our cause.

The day of the hearing, we gathered at the SPLC offices before going to the capitol. The lawyers had copies of all the relevant materials from the petition and from the original trial, and some of us

POLITICS BECOME PERSONAL

had brought some additional material. I brought a couple of letters from Dad to me to illustrate what an important positive influence he had been. At the capitol, we didn't have to wait long before being ushered into a large conference room. It was a rather dim room with dark paneling on the walls and a huge dark wooden conference table. The governor's chief counsel sat at the head of the long, somewhat oval table; he would relay the events of the hearing to the governor. Our group all sat along one side of the table or along the wall behind it. To my surprise, there were a few other people present, sitting or standing across from us in an adversarial posture. The head of the attorney general's capital crimes division was there. He stood the entire time, towering over the other side of the conference table with an expression that said we were wasting his time, and he wasn't happy about it. More surprising, at least to me, was one of the original prosecutors was there. It seemed highly unusual he would have any role in a hearing intended to determine whether someone deserved mercy, and more than one speaker among our group questioned what purpose he had there. Sitting against the wall on the other side of the room was a woman representing a victims' rights group. Since the victim had no family, she was intended to stand in for those who might have argued on his behalf. This also seemed strange, that for someone lacking any family or friends to object to a potential grant of mercy, they would seek out someone unrelated to make such an objection.

Our group was told to speak first. The lawyer made some introductions and made sure they received the written petition. I don't remember exactly what order we spoke in, but one by one, we made our pleas for mercy.

"The grey hairs on my chin attest that I've been around long enough to experience loss," John began, before asking that the chief counsel consider his own children and the other young friends and relatives who would be affected by this execution. He talked about his own history and how he nearly walked the same path before he turned his life around.

"I am not opposed to the death penalty," began the former pastor of my grandparents' church. He went on to talk about the change in my dad from before the crime to after he got saved. He was not opposed to the death penalty, but he was certain killing my dad would serve no positive purpose and would only end a fruitful ministry. The other ministers mostly had the same sentiments and reiterated the same points that killing my dad would gain nothing and cost much. The members of our family kept

POLITICS BECOME PERSONAL

their statements brief and simply begged for mercy for our family so we would not have to experience this loss. We had already suffered much, and we saw no reason to inflict this completely unnecessary loss on us.

When it was my turn to speak, I talked about how much I loved my dad. I talked about how much he meant to me and what a positive influence he was in my life. "My family members are hearing this for the first time," I said. "I was very close to walking the same road my dad walked. His influence is one of the biggest reasons I didn't go down that path." I read a little bit from the letters I had brought with me where Dad gave godly advice and shared scripture with me. "Dad always gives me some scripture or talks about Jesus," I said after I read one portion. I talked about how I didn't want to lose him and how even in prison, he had been a good father to me. I felt like somehow my words could be the difference between life and death for my dad; that maybe if I could just say the right thing, the chief counsel would be moved and press the governor for mercy. It's a feeling I wouldn't wish on anybody.

After our group was done making pleas and appeals for mercy, we discovered this really was an adversarial situation. The former prosecutor stood up and began making his own statement. "One of them said something like 'There but for the grace of God go I.' Well, Gary Brown did go there," he said. He had some files with him that I had assumed were notes or perhaps records from the original case. Instead, he pulled crime scene photos of the victim's body out of his folder and threw them down on the table. It was a display right out of a courtroom scene in a bad movie, complete with the theatric flair with which he threw down the photos so that they spread and slid on the table in front of the chief counsel.

I'm sure my face was somewhere between shock and eye roll as I thought. "This isn't an episode of *Law & Order*, and we aren't in a courtroom." In hindsight, I often wished I had said something to call him out on this ridiculous exhibition. It wouldn't have helped anything, but I might have enjoyed it.

As the gruesome pictures slid dramatically across the table, he said, "They talked about his positive impact on people, but what about the impact this scene had on the neighborhood children who found the body? Maybe he is reformed. I hope he goes to heaven." I felt like that was the most disingenuous statement I had ever heard. It didn't matter that seventeen years earlier, he had said on the record that Dad was the least culpable of the three, and it didn't matter Dad was the only one facing death. This prosecutor had gone well out of his way to try to convince everyone Dad needed to be killed.

After the prosecutor was done with his theatrics, the head of the capital crimes division had nothing significant to add. There was no doubt about his position and no doubt he had already spoken to the chief counsel outside the hearing. The victims' rights advocate was offered the chance to speak, but she declined. She didn't even really speak to say no but just sort of looked down and waved her hand. The look on her face said she was just as dismayed by this spectacle as I was. She was the only one in the room who seemed to possibly have been moved by everything our group had to say. Maybe as a victim's rights advocate she realized she didn't want to make victims of all of us.

The hearing was dismissed, and we filed out of the dark conference room. We awkwardly waited for the elevator with the prosecutor standing beside us. The man had driven down from Birmingham for a hearing that was supposed to be about mercy, a hearing he had no particular duty or reason to attend, so he could make a scene and try to ensure my dad was killed. Now we were supposed to nonchalantly make our exit as if nothing had happened. With miraculous restraint, none of us said anything, but I did decide to take the next elevator. Our group reconvened at the SPLC offices to have a bit of an after-action review. Everyone tried to act like it had gone well. I even made a quip about something ludicrous the head of the capital crimes division had recently said to the media. We talked a good game, but I don't think anyone felt good about what had just happened. We had been made into a circus. We had been made to endure this ordeal and it didn't make a bit of difference. This was the moment I first truly believed Dad was about to die.

○━━◆━━○

After the review at the SPLC offices, I made my way back to Huntsville. I was nearing the end of the final academic year of my long undergraduate career. I got back to my studies to the degree that I ever did. I kept up with the computer repair job I had at the time. I went back to student government association meetings and social activities and all the other things that kept me busy. Later in life, I would realize a lot of my perpetual busyness was a coping mechanism to keep me from dwelling too much on my life. As coping mechanisms go, that one was at least somewhat productive but still not the healthiest way to deal with my problems.

One of the classes I was taking was a senior design project on steroids, with three teams doing a real rocket design that would be presented to a panel of experts from government and industry. It was a great, intense class experience. I was a team leader, with the big final presentation scheduled for April 24; this was not the sort of thing one just skipped or made a lame excuse to get out of. The week prior, as we finished the written submission, I had to tell the team I would miss the presentation. I told a couple of friends on the team the reason, which completely shocked them. Then I had to tell the professor, which I did in an e-mail. He called my house; Sarah happened to be there and answered the phone. She assured him I was telling him the absolute truth about my situation. He let me know I could talk to the student services office at the university, and they would see I was excused from class activities or allowed to postpone them without having to talk to every professor I had about my situation. I didn't bother to use the service, but he was a good man and I appreciated that he was looking out for me.

As April 24 approached, I tried to be optimistic, and I tried to keep going with everyday life like everything was fine. Everything was not fine though, and in my heart, I knew there was no happy ending or eleventh-hour reprieve in store for us this time. On April 23, I made the trip to Atmore. Clemency had not been granted, and we had no indication that the governor might have some kind of change of heart. As I drove, our SPLC lawyer called me and, after a few brief words, told me she was sorry. "Don't be sorry yet," I told her. Where there's life, there's hope, I thought, but I wasn't feeling a lot of hope about this situation. I was struck by the cruel irony that the previous governor was probably going to grant clemency had there not been a stay of execution. Like the three Hebrew boys in the book of Daniel, I knew God could still save my dad, "But if not . . ."

The Monday after Easter 2003, three days before he would be executed, Dad had his final opportunity to preach at Life Row Church. What he shared was not a complete prepared sermon but more of a collection of thoughts and points he had on his mind. This message would be recorded and added to a tape of eulogies recorded after he was killed. One of the ministers who brought Life Row to the inmates would later say some of Dad's words touched him deeply and helped set him free from years of bondage. The last letter I received from my dad also mentioned Life Row Church. He said he now knew who would lead singing after he was gone, so he had nothing else to worry about. With his execution days away, he was concerned about the health of the church.

This final message is the last of the three tapes I have of my dad preaching. He talked a lot about what the disciples did just before Jesus was crucified and then after He had ascended into heaven. Just before Dad left his cell to go to the service, he felt the Holy Spirit say, "If you lift up Jesus, He'll draw men to Him." Dad started with some basic apologetics, talking about all that Jesus fulfilled and then the fact that the disciples never wavered after the resurrection even as they were arrested and executed: "Now I submit to you being a criminal all my life and a born-again believer now, praise God. So I'm not going confess that criminal stuff too much, but anyway. Don't you know, probably all of them would have took a plea bargain if they didn't know He'd shown up, rose up?" He talked about the apostle John whom he believed stayed with Jesus: "The Bible says if you try to save your life you'll lose it, okay? But those who lose it for Christ's sake will find it. Those ten disciples

I believe took off that night trying to save their life, right? I believe John stayed. Isn't it interesting that those ten all lost their life. John is the only one who lived to be ninety or whatever. Just something for you out there, for you theologians to think about." He went on to encourage the men to follow Jesus with their whole heart and serve God completely: "But if you're just gonna try Jesus, then you ain't gonna be saved. Because that's just, well, let me try this stuff out man see if it works. We can't come, okay, I'm gonna come to Christ so he can do all this stuff for me because if we come under that premise, we miss it. We missed it already. He can do all that stuff for you, but first you got to come based on what he already did at Calvary. When He gave his life, when He rose again. So, if you've come before and prayed this prayer, and went back to your cell and still do the same thing, act the same way, and talk the same way, and think the same things, brothers, it didn't take. Okay? You were just trying it, okay?" He talked about the importance of bearing godly fruit: "And let me tell you this too. If you've come to Christ and you've tried Jesus, the Bible says, by their fruit you shall know them, okay? And I'm not talking about people that mess up, because we all do that every day. But if you are continuously bearing fruit that's not of

God, well, brothers it didn't take. You need to come, tear that up, whatever it was you done last time, and do it again. You do it right, so that you can know that you know that you have eternal life." He ended the sermon with a final call to salvation: "And there's no hopeless or helpless feeling like there'll be when you stand before God and He says, 'What did you do with my Son?' 'Well, I read the Bible and stuff, but I have another opinion on that.' 'Depart from me I never knew you.' And it won't be because of what He did. It's because of us rejecting Him. I believe that tonight. I submit that to you, let the Holy Spirit deal with you as He may on that." Three days before he was killed, through God's grace, he was still doing what he could to lead others to Christ.

CHAPTER 8

A Different Kind of Freedom

> And God shall wipe away all
> tears from their eyes; and there
> shall be no more death, neither
> sorrow, nor crying, neither shall
> there be any more pain: for the
> former things are passed away.
> —Revelations 21:4 (KJV)

I began the morning of April 24, 2003, at the home of my dear friends in Atmore, near the prison. These friends would become like family to me, showing incredible grace and hospitality during an extremely difficult time. The first thing I saw as I opened my eyes that morning was an incredibly vivid rainbow cast across the entire ceiling of the bedroom. I was staying in the room of the only son in the family, and he had left a CD upside down on his desk beside the window. The sliver of bright sunlight entering between the window and the blinds struck the CD and reflected this incredible rainbow that I saw. To this day, I have never seen such a rainbow. In the Bible, the rainbow was the symbol of God's promise. Sometimes He uses the simplest of things to remind us of His love. A CD, left where the morning sun would strike it, seems like a trivial detail, but waking to the symbol of God's promise that morning let me know that whatever happened, He would comfort and sustain me. His grace would be enough.

I don't remember every detail of that day, but undeniably, some parts of it are seared into my memory. That morning, I drove up to the state capitol in Montgomery, accompanied by Dad's best friend John, in hopes of getting in to see the governor and maybe making one last impression that might lead him to grant clemency. I had spoken on the phone to the governor's chief counsel the day before.

"We don't want to make this difficult for the governor," he had said over the phone.

On the contrary, I wanted killing my father to be as difficult as possible for the governor. I wanted to make it so difficult that maybe he would just decide not to do it. The drive to Montgomery went by in a blur, and for the second time in my life, I walked in to the state capitol demanding to see the governor in hopes of saving my dad's life. It sounds bold and courageous, like I was staring down some overwhelming enemy like David going out to meet Goliath, but it really was nothing of the sort. It was an act of desperation, walking in to an old building to face down totally indifferent state bureaucrats. To be an enemy, the other party would have to care. Willful indifference is an entirely different kind of intimidation.

John spoke to the first secretary we encountered, and after a short wait, the governor's chief counsel emerged to meet us in the lobby. He explained that not only was the governor not at the capitol that day but he was also not even in the state. He was in Georgia at a conference. My naive idea that he was in his office agonizing over the decision of whether or not to spare a life was totally false. The talk of careful consideration seemed like nothing but political falsehood to us. Only he and God know whether the case even crossed his mind during that day—whether it was more than an inconsequential detail of state government to him. To us, it was the ultimate realization that the governor and those who advise him never had any intention of giving any real consideration to our petition for clemency. The machinery of death would move on under the cold indifference of those responsible for it.

"You should be spending the rest of this day with your dad," the governor's chief counsel said after explaining that the governor was away.

Our lawyer had said there was no indication the governor had even seen the clemency materials. During this time, the state attorney general had been appointed to a federal appeals court, and we would soon learn the governor's chief counsel had been tapped to be attorney general. Perhaps he didn't want to enter that role with a soft-on-crime clemency recommendation as one of his final acts. Perhaps the governor had already made it clear he would never grant clemency, and the chief counsel didn't bother him with minutiae like sparing a good man's life. Or perhaps the governor did see some of the materials and just didn't care. Whatever the case, that trip to Montgomery was fruitless. As far as we could tell, the spectacle the chief counsel had presided over at the clemency hearing was nothing but a farce. We made the drive back to Atmore to spend the rest of the afternoon in one final visit.

CHILD OF GRACE: A DEATH ROW STORY

On a typical visitation day, the visitor's yard at Holman is busy and loud, with many inmates and their families all in the one large room, the industrial fans running full time to keep the temperature reasonable. Thursday is not a normal visitation day at the prison, and the Thursday of an execution is anything but typical. Just like the prior execution date, we had the visitor's yard to ourselves; the only sounds other than our talk were the occasional passersby in the hallways around the yard. There was a distinct pall over the whole area as we sat in the middle of the yard. Dad had been there a long time and had a good relationship with many of the corrections officers. Some of them truly considered him a friend. This day was exceptionally difficult for them as they were required to be professional and do their jobs, even though their jobs required them to be part of killing a friend. The first time we had gone through the routine of an execution day had been a lot different. For one thing, executions in the electric chair took place just after midnight, but executions under lethal injection took place at six o'clock in the evening so everything happened much earlier in the day. For me, leading up to the first execution date, there was never a time when I felt he would actually be killed that day. Even when we finally got the word of the stay the first time, my reaction was fairly muted because I just knew it was coming. I believe the Holy Spirit was telling my soul the time had not yet come, so I did not have the feelings of dread one would expect. This time, however, I had really known since the clemency hearing it was going to happen. I had talked a good game about the various possibilities, but my heart knew the truth. And on that day, the feeling was much different, particularly after our disheartening trip to Montgomery.

Our final visit seemed to last for ages and yet end too soon. There were lots of stories, lots of scripture being read, lots of prayer, and lots of old hymns being sung. Everyone tried to express all the things they wanted to say before the end. One of my aunts started talking about wishing she had been a better sister, but that was quickly called off as counterproductive. And so everyone tried to keep the mood as positive as possible despite the circumstances. There was even some laughter through some of the stories and lighthearted conversation that afternoon. Dad and I talked about music and cars and school and all the other topics we often covered. He talked about Jesus, grace, and forgiveness as he so often did. I tried not to think about the things he wouldn't be around for, like my graduation coming just a couple of weeks later or a wedding I was already sure would be on the horizon. He wouldn't have been there in person, but I had hoped he might be around to see the pictures and talk to about all of it. Late in the afternoon, we were interrupted by the news that Dad's lawyer was on the phone. Appeals and petitions continue right up to the last minute in these cases, and though we knew there was not likely to be any good news, there was still technically some hope of a reprieve. While he was taking the call, the rest of us spent those few minutes in prayer. Dad's body language on his way back told us everything we needed to know. He confirmed his final appeal had been denied, and the execution would move forward as planned.

We all tried to appreciate the final little bit of time we had together. We took communion and sang hymns. The cloud of darkness hanging over us was hard to ignore now, and the tears were hard to hold back. I wanted to believe that, somehow, the governor would make a last-minute clemency call, but I knew there was no realistic hope left. The last minutes went by in a flash, and suddenly, several officers entered the room and said the words we had been dreading: "Gary, it's time to go." We all stood up, and tearful hugs began. I wish I could say we shared a final moment worthy of a movie script, but it was really anticlimactic. Neither of us was quite sure what to say. He looked in to my eyes, gave a bit of a shrug, and said, "I guess this is it." We hugged, whispered "I love you" to each other while we embraced, and that was it. He and his spiritual adviser, the same Mennonite pastor who had been there with us a year earlier, were ushered to the death cell where he would spend the next hour waiting to be taken to the execution chamber. That was the last time I got to see my dad on this earth.

Dad and his spiritual adviser spent that time in the death cell talking about God's grace. Dad told him he wished he could have served Jesus better, but the pastor told Dad God's grace is sufficient in our weaknesses. They talked some about heaven and what it might be like. MercyMe's famous song "I Can Only Imagine" was still new at that time, and it was one of Dad's favorites. They talked about Dad's statement to family that God wasn't wrong, a reassurance to place our trust in God even when we don't understand what He is doing or why. Dad had refused a real last meal and instead ate an ice cream sandwich from a vending machine. After about an hour, the officers once again came and said, "It's time." The pastor read Jude 24–25 (NIV): "To him who is able to keep you from stumbling and to present you before his glorious presence without fault and with great joy—to the only God our Savior be glory, majesty, power and authority, through Jesus Christ our Lord, before all ages, now and forevermore! Amen." They prayed for God's grace, strength, and peace to be with Dad. Then he was led away to the execution chamber while the pastor made his long walk out of the prison.

Dad was seen talking with the officers leading him away from the death cell to the execution chamber. I was told later he was sharing Jesus with the officers even as they were leading him away to be killed. Nobody but the officers and God know exactly what was said, but I fully believe he was continuing to bear witness for his Savior and telling them God's grace is sufficient no matter what happens. I believe Dad's last moments were spent sharing the good news of Jesus Christ, even with those who were about to take his life. They led Dad to the execution chamber where he was strapped to a gurney and prepared to become the second man killed by lethal injection by the state of Alabama.

A DIFFERENT KIND OF FREEDOM

John and one family member would be the ones to witness the execution, along with a few reporters. They had to leave the visiting yard when Dad and his spiritual advisor went back to the death cell and were instructed to wait at a nearby motel for the prison van to come pick them up. They took a slow drive back to the prison complex and then followed a black vehicle with the words "Mobile Forensic Department" around to the back of the prison. The vehicle was there to take the body; it seemed particularly cruel to have to follow it in. They had to wait in the van for a few minutes before another prison van, carrying members of the press, arrived. Apparently, someone had told quite a joke because the officer driving that van was in the midst of uproarious laughter.

They were ushered into a dark room with the curtain drawn. The execution chamber was well lit, and the gurney with my dad already on it was visible through the curtain. Members of the press sat on either side of them. Eventually, the curtain was pulled back, and they could see him clearly. There were two corrections officers in the chamber, one on either side of the gurney. One had a clear look of pain on his face; the other just stared at the ground. The chaplain was also there, looking equally distraught. The warden entered the room, picked up a microphone, and read the execution order. The warden asked if he had any last words, but the family present had signaled not to say anything. Dad honored that wish and told the warden no but later mouthed "Forgive them" and "Go with God" as his unofficial last words. The warden then left the room followed by the two officers. One of them stopped and squeezed his arm goodbye. The chaplain was the last to leave the room. It sounded liked he said "I love you, Gary," before he turned and walked out.

They began pumping the three-drug cocktail of death into his veins. His eyes closed, he jerked a couple of times, and entered what looked like a deep sleep. After nineteen minutes, his color left him, the curtain was closed, and he was pronounced dead. The clinical and professional appearance of the whole proceeding did not assuage the brutal fact that the agents of the state had killed my father. Dad had showed no trace of bitterness or anger throughout the execution. His face was peaceful and calm. John said at the end, "I hope one day, I am able to die with as much dignity as Gary Brown did."

A DIFFERENT KIND OF FREEDOM

There was a time when I wished I had been there with him in his final moments. I know now it would have been a mistake, and being haunted by that experience would have done me no good. I wanted to be there for him and with him, but he believed I should not be there. This was definitely a time that father knew best. After our final goodbye in the visitation yard, I returned to the home of our dear friends with some other friends and family members. The pastor who acted as spiritual adviser would later join us there after spending the hour in the death cell with Dad. Our friends in Atmore are one of these families who live on the same property as some of their extended family, so we were gathered in the living room of their parents, waiting for news. We sat around sharing idle chatter for an hour or so, talking about what I would do after college and that sort of thing. I even stepped out onto the porch to take a call from a classmate who was telling me how the final presentation for our senior design team had gone. He was also a good friend; he knew where I was and that I would like to know about the presentation.

"We're about thirty minutes from good news or bad news," I told him.

Uncle Leonard stepped onto the porch after me, thinking maybe I had gotten some last-minute news about my dad. As we stood there looking at the rural countryside, I told him I was glad my grandfather, his father, hadn't lived to experience this pain. Leonard agreed.

Back inside the house, the minutes ticked by like hours. Then the call finally came that it was over. Some of us cried while others just seemed numb. One was stretched out on the floor bawling. I just sat there with no real reaction at first. As the others started to filter over to our friends' house for dinner, I snuck away into an extra bedroom. There, by myself, the floodgate of tears opened. I wept like never before and never since. I cried out to God, I yelled "Why?" through the tears over and over. Why did they have to kill my dad? Keeping him in prison wasn't enough? Why did God not do anything to stop it? Why could we not have a miracle? I even made a bawling, incoherent phone call to Sarah. I was inconsolable and sobbing uncontrollably. I don't know how long I was in that bedroom, crying those agonized tears and crying out to God, but eventually, I begged Him for peace. Philippians 4:7 tells us of the peace of God that transcends all understanding. I can tell you His peace is as real as any tangible thing in this world. I cried out for peace, prayed this verse, and He gave it to me. His peace swept over me in a wave I could

A DIFFERENT KIND OF FREEDOM

physically feel. In an instant, I was comforted by the Almighty God; I felt real peace in the arms of Jesus. The tears stopped, and I felt at ease. I called Sarah and told her I planned to come back to Huntsville later that night. She would later talk about the two radically different phone calls she got from me in a short time that evening. Then I went and joined the rest of our family and friends for dinner.

Dinner that night was surprisingly good and uneventful given the tragedy we had just experienced. Everyone managed to stay composed, our gracious hosts serving us and making us feel at home. I spoke with the pastor who had been with my dad, and he told me a little of what they had talked about. I asked him how this could be God's will.

"Suffering was not part of God's plan. God's plan was the paradise man started in, but man's sin has led to every kind of pain and suffering." The pastor's words were certainly a comfort to me. That day, God had surrounded me with his saints, and they were a blessing to me.

The Gospel of Luke chapter 23 tells us when Jesus was crucified, there were two thieves crucified alongside him. One of them recognized Jesus was the Messiah and cried out to Him for mercy: "Then he said, 'Jesus, remember me when you come into your kingdom.' Jesus answered him, 'Truly I tell you, today you will be with me in paradise'" (Luke 23:42–43, NIV). The prosecutors, the leaders, the gathered mob, the system—they all thought it was just for this thief to die. They thought they had prevailed. In his final moments, the thief on the cross received the greatest gift anyone can be given: eternity in heaven with our Lord and Savior Jesus Christ.

Before his final day, Dad had really believed he would be set free in earthly terms. There were some legal technicalities that made it a possibility, such as the nuance that a commutation to a regular life sentence would make him parole-eligible right away and even some circumstances like a previous conviction that seemed to be missing from the record that otherwise would have hampered the possibility of parole. There had been words of prophecy from different people about freedom, and one of them even saw the writing of a book. God wasn't wrong. Dad is completely free now; it was just a different kind of freedom than our carnal selves had hoped for.

CHAPTER 9

My Life After His Death

> Therefore, since we are surrounded by such a great cloud of witnesses, let us throw off everything that hinders and the sin that so easily entangles.
> —Hebrews 12:1 (NIV)

After our execution night dinner and some tearful goodbyes, I made the long late-night drive back to Huntsville, fueled by Mountain Dew and loud music to help me make it home after the most emotionally draining day of my life. I thought about what would come next, whether I would keep in touch with some of the people I didn't really know apart from my dad and what would be missing from my life. There would be no more long early-morning drives to Atmore to visit the prison. I had been to Holman

Correctional Facility for the last time. There would be no more handmade cards from Dad at every holiday. There would be no more expensive collect phone calls from prison. There would be no more letters. After my granddad had passed away, I had a few moments where I had seen something interesting and thought, "I'll have to tell Papa about that," but then would remember he was gone. It was not quite the same after Dad died. There was no way to forget they had killed him.

I woke up midmorning on that Friday after getting home in the wee hours of the morning. My roommates kept a thoughtful distance. Sarah was there for me, but I was still living in that wave of peace that God had given me and didn't need much comforting. What could she really have said? "I'm sorry the state just killed your dad"? She was there for me, and that was more than enough. That afternoon, I took a final exam. It was one of the easier ones, so I did fine on it without much preparation. I don't know why I hadn't at least postponed it until the next week when I would take the rest of my finals. That night, we went bowling with friends. As far as I knew, only one of them was aware of what I had gone through the night before. I acted like everything was normal, and by God's grace, I felt pretty normal.

MY LIFE AFTER HIS DEATH

I received an inheritance from Dad. It was in a paper grocery sack. When I got back home with it, I left the top of the sack rolled down. For one thing, I needed to concentrate on passing my final, but mostly, I didn't quite feel ready to open it and go through it. The press solved that problem for me. I made the mistake of reading a news article a well-meaning person e-mailed me, and there in the article was every detail of my inheritance. The Bibles, the *Strong's Concordance*, the *Vine's Bible Dictionary*, the wooden cross, the set of prison whites—it was all in there. I'm not sure why the press even had access to personal items left as an inheritance for a grieving son, and I certainly can't imagine why it would be considered newsworthy.

The following week, I took my remaining final exams and managed to pass them all. I had two classes to complete over the summer but was allowed to walk in commencement on Mother's Day of 2003. I was the first in my family to walk across the stage for a university degree—actually two degrees in my case. I received some personal words of congratulations from some of the university administrators and one of my department chairs as I made my way across the stage. I think they were just glad I managed to finish. It is hard to imagine the emotional rollercoaster of my grandmother losing her son and, a few weeks later, watching her adopted son walk across the stage. The whole thing was surreal.

In the days following the execution, I also started to receive some letters and e-mails expressing condolences and sharing what a positive influence my dad had been. There was a memorial service in Atmore that I didn't get to attend because of my exam schedule and another in Birmingham in which I did participate. Members of the Life Row Church recorded eulogies that were included with a tape of Dad's final sermon from the Monday before he was killed. To my knowledge, almost all those men have since been killed or died in prison. Having friends on death row means consistently checking the news to discover someone you know is being killed. None of those men were beyond the reach of God's grace.

The letters and eulogies all had a common theme: God's grace and the light that shined through my dad. The pastor of the church that sponsored the Life Row ministers had gone with them into the prison a few times.

"I did not expect to receive the rich blessing from the death row inmates that I found," he wrote. "Gary was always a blessing. His gentle spirit, kind words, profound truths, and sincere passion for Christ were always evident."

One of the Life Row ministers wrote, "He represented a level of stability and faithfulness that comes from a strong relationship with our Savior . . . I soaked up all of Gary's wisdom that I could before he went home."

These and many other words that were shared with us during that time were a great comfort to me. Dad had really made a difference in many people's lives despite his circumstances. The cards I treasured most came from death row. More than twenty of the men had written little notes and signed a few cards. Once again, the men who were supposed to be the worst of the worst were sending words of encouragement, quoting scripture, and sharing what my dad had meant to them. Most of those men are gone now, but I believe they are in heaven and I believe my dad was a positive influence for Christ in their lives.

CHILD OF GRACE: A DEATH ROW STORY

That fall, I started graduate school. I went to business school and would graduate with a master of science in management of technology two years later. By the end of the fall, I was hired for another engineering job that would really begin my career in the aerospace industry. Better than all that, Sarah and I got married on December 13, 2003. God had blessed me with a wonderful woman who was perfect for me. We had met in a pretty unlikely way, which also cemented our status as total nerds: we met on the way to a space conference at MIT. She was attending another university when we met, and the next year, she transferred to UAH. The wedding was small, with only close family on either side and our dear friends from Atmore. Dad's spiritual adviser spoke at the wedding, and the vows were administered by another minister who had gotten to know Dad. God had richly blessed me that fall, and when the new year started, I was intent on walking with Him.

About a year after Dad died, I slowly began to come to terms with all that had happened. God gave me that overwhelming peace I had asked Him for, but the time had come for me to start to process the events of my life, mourn losses, deal with difficult things in my life, and learn to forgive. Forgiveness is one of the most difficult things Jesus called us to do but also one of the most necessary for our own well-being. Forgiveness can also be a process, and we often have to ask the Holy Spirit to help us continue to forgive someone. I worked to forgive the governor and his chief counsel and the prosecutor who had come to the clemency hearing. I forgave family members whom I felt had somehow done wrong by me. I forgave Dad for going so far wrong that he wound up on death row in the first place. Hardest of all, I tried to forgive myself for my many mistakes and for how badly I had treated some people who didn't deserve it in the least, like my granddad. Slowly, month after month and year after year, God brought healing in my heart and mind. Early in my marriage, I would get upset any time I saw news about my dad specifically or executions in general, and for years, I would break down in tears on the anniversary of his death. I would become withdrawn and distant with my wife during these spells, which I know was hard on her. Eventually, God's grace brought me to a place of healing where I no longer struggled with things people would say or that I saw on the news. He also delivered me from some of the lingering addiction I had struggled with during those years. That doesn't mean life was easy. Several people in my family died before their time. Uncle Charles and Aunt Mary on my mom's side died young. Uncle James died young. My cousin Jeffrey who had been close to me as a young teen had slipped into hard drugs by the time I finished high school; he died of a heroin overdose before I turned thirty. My grandmother, suffering from anxiety attacks and dementia, spent three years in a nursing home before she passed away. God's grace was sufficient to carry me through all those struggles.

The sin that is most difficult to overcome, the one that is often most insidious and most damaging, is pride. Foolish pride had made my college years more difficult than they needed to be, and it would strike again in my midtwenties. After I finished my business degree, I decided to start a small business. There was nothing inherently wrong with that, but I was not really walking where God directed. It started out well enough, but foolish pride led me to overextend.

"God wouldn't bring us this far to let us fail now," Sarah and I told ourselves.

That was a lie of course. God hadn't brought us there. Rather, we had recklessly brought ourselves there, and He would certainly allow that to fail in order to bring us back to His will. When the Great Recession started, the business failed spectacularly, and since we had overextended, what could have been mitigated as neutral or a small loss ended up being a tremendous financial loss. In the same time period, I had gotten involved in an unrelated partnership that also led to harm. The business was fine, and in fact I would continue that kind of work for a while after the partnership fell apart, but I should have seen from the beginning that this partner would bring bad news.

Once again, foolish pride made me think it would somehow be all right and that it couldn't really be that bad. In fact, it was that bad, that partner leaving me holding the bag for problems in the business, costing me a great deal of money. At the end of 2009, the first business was in full collapse, the partnership was showing obvious signs of trouble, and I got laid off from my day job as an engineer. It was easily the lowest point in our marriage. I could certainly blame the recession or the partner for all those troubles, but I know my foolish pride was what put me in that position in the first place. Pride is one of Dante's seven deadly sins and also one of the most difficult to overcome.

CHILD OF GRACE: A DEATH ROW STORY

By the grace of God, what the enemy means for destruction can be turned to good. The beginning of 2010 was a low point that had us on the edge of financial ruin, but God's grace was big enough to see us through our mistakes. We finally closed the doors on the failing business, saving us time and stress, if not money. We would eventually be able to settle on our obligations there. The trouble that sprang from the bad partnership was taken care of so quickly and favorably it had the air of *deus ex machina*, even if it did cost quite a bit of money to right the wrongs. I got a new day job that started in the spring of 2010, a well-paying aerospace job that has been by far the best engineering job I've ever had.

Miraculously, by the beginning of 2012, we had overcome all the financial setbacks and were doing quite well financially. Our turnaround was so swift and miraculous that it bolstered my wife's faith in a way nothing before ever had. The incredible boost in our faith was worth all the self-inflicted hardship. Sarah often says we would have lost that money one way or another, with some other venture or in investments that crashed in the recession. Neither of us thinks too much about it. It's only money, and God can provide as much of that as we need. We learned and grew tremendously as we came out of those problems; we learned about ourselves, about what was really important to us, and about depending on Jesus. I know part of the turnaround came when we had gotten back into a great church after a period of rarely going. We also made a choice to continue tithing on our day job incomes and not discount all the losses we were taking from the other ventures. It is hard to overstate how important it is to stay in community with other believers. Hebrews 10:24–25 (NIV) says, "And let us consider how we may spur one another on toward love and good deeds, not giving up meeting together, as some are in the habit of doing, but encouraging one another—and all the more as you see the Day approaching."

Since that low point, God has continued to bless us far beyond anything we could have hoped for. We have had the great honor of sharing His love on mission trips in Latin America. It was on a trip to the Amazon region that I got some opportunities to speak, where I was able to share my dad's testimony for the first time. I was speaking at a local ministry school for indigenous teenagers and young adults. There, in a small structure with a dirt floor, being translated first into Spanish and then into the Ticuna language, I was able to share my testimony. My new church friends didn't realize it at the time, but that was a huge breakthrough for me. I had never before had enough courage to speak openly about it. Not surprisingly, they were somewhat shocked to hear about my background. These days, I actually get a little enjoyment out of the reaction people have when I share my testimony. "But you're the most normal guy I know" and "I never would have guessed" are typical of the reactions. God's grace has brought me so far that people have a hard time believing some of the things from my past. Our church has continued to be a wonderful community of godly people who have treated us like family whether we deserved it or not.

In October of 2012, we had that experience that will remove every bit of pride you have: our daughter was born. Two years later, almost to the day, our son was born. Nothing will humble you like kids. I like to complain about all their messy, noisy antics, but there are few greater joys in life than these precious little ones. In 2014, I finished my PhD in engineering management, a field that combines systems engineering and organizational management. I've been teaching a class at the university since then. When my mom was going into labor with me in jail, nobody would have thought I would be called Dr. Brown one day. God has been so good to me; even when I least deserved it, His grace has been there for me. He has carried me through the hard times and blessed me beyond measure.

In 2016, after learning about it from a college friend, I began volunteering with Kairos Prison Ministry. Some people were surprised I would ever want to set foot in a prison again. I was concerned about how I would feel when I first walked through the gate, whether I would have some kind of flashback or completely freak out, but it turned out I was as comfortable as I could be back in prison ministering to some of the least of these. As is always the case, I've ended up being more blessed by the men in white than they have by me. Prison worship services are now some of my absolute favorite times. God's grace has brought me full circle.

I don't want to leave you with the impression that my dad was perfect or should be nominated for sainthood for anything he did after he accepted Jesus. Even after he was delivered from his addictions and got past his spiritual dry spell, he made plenty of mistakes. Sometimes he made selfish requests of friends or family, sometimes he interpreted scripture in a way that seemed a bit self-serving, and sometimes he was bitten by the pride bug himself. I don't want you to finish this book thinking I should be nominated for sainthood either or that I am some kind of exceptional person overcoming great odds to achieve great success. I make mistakes all the time and I am far from exceptional. Neither my dad nor I deserve to be saints or celebrities or highly honored people. We are both broken, deeply flawed people in need of the Savior.

We are simply children of grace.

AFTERWORD

I remember my affliction and my wandering, the bitterness and the gall. I well remember them, and my soul is downcast within me. Yet this I call to mind and therefore I have hope: Because of the Lord's great love we are not consumed, for his compassions never fail. They are new every morning; great is your faithfulness. I say to myself, 'The Lord is my portion; therefore I will wait for him.' The Lord is good to those whose hope is in him, to the one who seeks him; it is good to wait quietly for the salvation of the Lord.
—Lamentations 3:19–26 (NIV)

AFTERWORD

I wrote this book, with all its painful memories and embarrassing confessions, first, because I believe the Holy Spirit called me to do so and, second, because I believe this story could help others. If you picked up this book because you wanted to know some details about prison or executions, I hope you got a lot more than that out of it. If you read to the end, I hope you have realized God's grace is big enough to save anybody. If you were hard-hearted and thought salvation was only for those who lived a clean and holy life from the start, or some people were just not worthy of salvation, I hope you have realized even the worst of the worst are not beyond God's grace. If you were down on yourself and believed you had gone too far and done too much wrong to turn back to God now, I hope you saw even men on death row were not too far gone to be saved. No matter what you have done or how long you have travelled the wrong path, you are not beyond the reach of God's grace. And finally, if you picked up this book and don't know Jesus Christ as your Lord and Savior, I hope you will pray a prayer like my dad did sitting in the county jail: "Jesus, I realize I have completely wasted most of my life so far, and I am oh so tired of running from you. Regardless of what happens from now on, I don't want to run from you any longer. I want to surrender my life to you now. Please set me free from this unbearable burden of guilt and sin." Romans 10:9 (NIV) says, "If you declare with your mouth, 'Jesus is Lord,' and believe in your heart that God raised him from the dead, you will be saved." You can acknowledge Jesus Christ was the Son of God, the second person in the Holy Trinity, and died for your sins, conquered death, and rose again to ascend to the right hand of the Father. If you believe it in your heart and pray for forgiveness, you will be saved. Make that prayer your own, and confess whatever you need to as you ask Jesus to become your personal Lord and Savior. You will never regret it.

NOTES

Gary, Leon, Sara, Sarah, and Mrs. Christmas are the only real names in this book. All the other names have been changed to protect the innocent (and the guilty). This is a book about God's grace, and I don't want that to get overshadowed by any people famous or otherwise. I also don't want to cause any harm to people who might feel they were portrayed in a negative light. I don't intend to damage or hurt anyone with this book.

You may wonder where I got all the information presented here. Some of it, particularly from Dad's early life and his first few years in prison, was from a whopping forty-two-page version of his testimony that he typed out but never distributed. Some of it was from letters sent to me by the various people involved. Some of it was from the clemency petition and trial transcripts and related sources. Some of it is simply my recollection of events. This book is not

NOTES

impervious to any kind of minor error of fact, but it is as accurate as it could reasonably be.

This is not an explicitly anti–death penalty book. However, just as true accounts of the realities of war can leave someone feeling a book or film is antiwar, true accounts of the realities of capital punishment are likely to come across as anti–death penalty. Ultimately, this is not a political book; it is a book about God's incredible grace.

ABOUT THE AUTHOR

Son of a criminal sentenced to death, Dr. Chris Brown writes from his extensive experience of loving someone through failure and finding grace in the midst of trials. Chris has shared his message of hope both at home and abroad, with free men and convicts, all believing they are too far gone, too lost, too broken to be accepted and lovingly restored by God. Chris' unique experience and love for God, who also walked a road to execution, make his message not only authentic but also life changing for those who receive it.

CPSIA information can be obtained
at www.ICGtesting.com
Printed in the USA
BVHW081924171218
535790BV00010B/795/P

9 781644 162743